Twitter

for Business

Success

Everything Business Owners
Need to Know About Twitter

Made Easy!

WITHDRAWN

Nicky Kriel

How to Twitter for Business Success

Published by

THE OTHER PUBLISHING COMPANY
www.otherpublishingcompany.com

ISBN: 978-0-9573191-5-8

Cover Design by Deana Riddle
Author's photo by Samantha Falconer
Book Design by BookStarter

How To Twitter For Business Success

Nicky Kriel is passionate about empowering, inspiring and educating business owners to use Social Media to grow their business. She uses her background in marketing and sales to help businesses to incorporate Social Media into their business strategy. As a Master NLP Practitioner she teaches people to engage and to remember the "social" aspect of Social Networking—it isn't all about tools and technology, but about people and relationships. Based in Guildford, Surrey in England, she has worked with businesses ranging from solopreneurs to multinational companies helping them to use Social Media more strategically. In the last few years she has help hundreds of business owners to start their Twitter journey and to use Twitter successfully as a marketing and public relations tool.

www.nickykriel.com

Foreword

By Dee Blick, FCIM, Chartered Marketer, author of the No. 1 bestseller: *The Ultimate Small Business Marketing Book*

If you're interested in reading this book I guess that either you want to understand more about Twitter and are wondering whether you should join in and start Tweeting or you're already on Twitter and are interested in picking up some new tips.

Or perhaps you're using Twitter successfully, nicely building up your following and developing your voice, but you're curious and keen to learn more. Perhaps you are wondering what else could you be doing on Twitter to extend your reach, and what are the useful tools that you're not aware of but should be? Or, you may simply be asking, is there room for improvement in the way you are using Twitter?

Maybe you have dabbled with Twitter before but decided it's not for you. In hindsight you can now see that you were to blame for this and not Twitter, so you're thinking it's time to start afresh but this time with all the essential up-to-date Twitter know-how.

So if building a successful, effective and enduring presence on Twitter is on your marketing list, this book is definitely the right one for you.

You will not be disappointed.

With so many social media marketing experts dominating the online landscape today, it can be hard to sort out the genuine bonafide experts that you really should pay close attention to, from their less experienced counterparts who have found a voice but one that's lacking in substance, expertise and experience. Nicky Kriel is definitely a genuine social media marketing expert of the very best kind; an expert with many years business experience who practices what she preaches on Twitter, with a loyal following who benefit from her expertise, her blogs and her tips that she freely gives on a daily basis.

Nicky works with small businesses every day, helping them to develop their Twitter strategy on a one-to-one basis and through her sell-out training events and webinars. She understands how small businesses should use Twitter, the mistakes they make, the challenges they face and ultimately what they have to do in order to become successful on Twitter.

What you get in this superb ultimate guide to Twitter is page after page of fantastic Twitter tips, expert common sense and an absolute mine of useful and practical Twitter know-how, all written in a charming and conversational style. You will find each chapter a pleasure to read. Make sure you have a pen and notepad to hand because the information in this book is solid gold with the power to transform your business if you are willing to put the effort in.

Dee Blick, FCIM

Contents

Why you should be using Twitter

Twitter will help your business to:

- Build brand awareness
- Connect with like-minded people
- Share information
- Get information
- Attract new customers
- Remind existing customers that you are still there
- Engage with customers
- Network
- Promote your blog
- Show your expertise
- Drive traffic to your website
- Recruit new staff
- Find news
- Keep up to date with your industry
- Share links to photos, videos and articles
- Improve Public Relations
- Connect with journalists

- Promote courses and products
- Improve customer service
- Be found by Search Engines
- Listen to what people are saying about you

BUT most importantly...

You should be using Twitter, because Twitter is FUN!

To Tweet or not to Tweet?

That's the question everyone running a business should be asking themselves.

Social Media, which includes *Facebook*, *Twitter* and *YouTube,* is growing rapidly. It has overtaken porn as the number one internet activity. The number of people who use any of the big three social media platforms is simply phenomenal.

So, what is Twitter? Probably the best way to describe Twitter is that it is like texting, but instead of sending a text to someone's phone, you send it to the web. Each Tweet is less than 140 characters and becomes in effect a mini webpage or a micro blog. Twitter is a great way of spreading information, news, commentary and even gossip.

People talk about things on Twitter. News gets spread around the world within minutes with Twitter and often breaks on Twitter first. Recently New Yorkers read Tweets about an earthquake on the East Coast, thirty seconds before they actually felt it.

60% of Twitter's 140 million active monthly participants use their mobile devices to Tweet— so imagine how quickly news of a business's good service can be spread around, and equally how quickly news of bad service can be passed on to others. And consider this: 90% of people trust peer recommendations, only 14% trust advertisements.

Bearing all the above in mind—ask yourself—do you want people to be recommending you? Do you want to harness the power of Twitter? The answer has to be, 'Yes!' If you run your own business, wouldn't you want to increase the exposure of your company? Wouldn't you want to increase the number of customers? Wouldn't you want to build up good relationships with existing customers? Of course you would. And the good news is that all of this costs you nothing. Nothing—except your time.

I know just how useful Twitter can be because I have tried it myself and it works. In December 2009 things were very quiet for my business. At this time people were telling me about Twitter but I'd done nothing about it and then one day I decided to sit down and work out what Twitter was all about. In fact, I had first taken some tentative steps back in August, but I had been a little intimidated by the Twitter Stream and the strange abbreviations it used so I had abandoned the experiment within days. But on that December day when I finally decided to learn how to use Twitter once and for all, I discovered a new a very powerful medium that revolutionised my life and my way of thinking.

Since then Twitter has dramatically changed my business and I would definitely rate it as the best business decision I ever took.

I had my first business enquiry via Twitter within two weeks. Within three months of being on Twitter, I had over 1,500 followers.

Twitter is the biggest source of referral traffic to my website and it helps me to be found on Google and all kinds of web searches. I now have more visitors to my website on a daily basis than I used to get in a month. I get new business in each week, which I can directly attribute to Twitter alone.

But for me the best part of Twitter has been the people I have met and the relationships that have developed from it. The world is full of interesting people and if you are genuine and open to possibilities, you will be amazed at how many doors can open up for you.

I have met some fascinating people: I have found myself chatting with self-made millionaires and world-class speakers and people I would never normally have access to—such as an author I really respect, who even invited me to her house for lunch. A single Tweet about starting a Speakers' Club gave me a long list of people who were interested in joining; most of my radio interviews started on Twitter and (just to show you how versatile this medium is) I have even dated someone I met through Twitter.

So, if you are ready to find out more about how Twitter can be used to grow your business, this book is for you and will help you on your way.

The Perks and Pitfalls of Twitter

The Perks

You connect with a far greater audience —than you could by networking or asking for referrals. Networking is fun and can give you a buzz if you are extroverted, but exactly how many people can you meet at each meeting? And how much of your valuable time does networking take up? Networking online (i.e. by using Twitter) can allow you to make real connections with real people. And it is more time efficient.

Raise your profile both online and offline— Have you ever had strangers walk up to you and say, '*You are ..., aren't you*?' And then found out that they know exactly what business you are in because they follow you on Twitter? Have you ever been invited to do podcasts about your business? Or radio interviews? Have you ever been quoted by someone else as an expert? Well, all these things are all possible with Twitter and without spending a penny on public relations. I know because they have all happened to me and they could be happening to you too!

Potential clients can get a taste of what you are like before they commit—Your personality comes through even in 140 characters and potential customers can sample bite-size pieces of what you offer. You build rapport before even meeting or talking to people. People feel connected to you if they can read your thoughts and opinions, see pictures of you, hear your voice or watch a video of you.

Meet like-minded people—I have met so many supportive wonderful people on Twitter who are willing me on to succeed. Like attracts like. If you stay true to yourself and are helpful and friendly you will attract the same type of people. There are many people out there who will like what you are doing if your intentions are good.

Learn about your industry and how to take your business forward—Twitter has provided me with a wealth of information. There is so much information about how to do almost anything and most of it is freely available. The Twitter community love to rally around and help people who ask questions.

The Pitfalls

It's a marathon, not a sprint—Things don't tend to happen instantly. For Social Media to work for you, you need to be part of the community, which means you need to show up consistently. You don't need to spend hours each day on Twitter, but you do need to commit to being there. You need to think about building long-term relationships.

You can't hide behind a corporate image— People do business with people they know, like and trust and you will get further by revealing your true personality than by using business-talk and stiff marketing language.

There is no simple automated formula— If someone suggests you automate everything, please don't pay attention to them. There is no substitute for personality. You need to build up your own quality network, engage with your audience as a person and not be a robot (more about this later). Anyone who thinks that an automated feed of marketing messages is going to bring them business needs to consider this: How would you respond to someone continuously bombarding you with sales messages? Would you rush out to buy from them? Or would you find a way to shut off the noise?

You need to be conscious that what you say on Twitter is public—What you broadcast online becomes public and visible to a large number of people. Don't put up posts you wouldn't want your family to read or that you wouldn't want to see as a headline in a newspaper. Tweets have been used in court! Remember, you are publishing online. You always need to be conscious of how you market yourself. For example, if you are a life-coach, telling people you are depressed is probably not going to help your business.

It is easy to get overwhelmed—It is very easy to be overpowered by the sheer quantity of Tweets on Twitter, the constant flow of information and the feeling that you are never going to get on top of it all! So to avoid this pitfall, start with a big picture of where you would like to be and have a clear intention in mind of what you want to achieve.

There might seem to be a lot to learn, but remember—you start every journey with a single step.

A winning formula for using Twitter

Quality Network

You need to decide who your ideal audience is before you start. It is far more important to build a quality network than to focus on numbers. Anyone who thinks that the goal of Twitter is to accumulate followers is missing the point. It is like thinking that the purpose of going to a networking meeting is to collect as many business cards as possible and that somehow you are going to get a prize for getting the highest number. The point of Tweeting as a small business owner is to use it as a tool to grow your business. This goes beyond *collecting* people—it means *building* relationships. You may need to build numbers when you start (because there is no point in Tweeting if no one is paying attention to your Tweets) but you want the right people in your network, rather than amassing a collection of random people. Quality is far more important than quantity.

Quality Content

Always provide quality content whenever you Tweet. You'll do this if you start with your reader in mind. Always think about to whom you are Tweeting and what impact you want your Tweet to have. Content isn't just your updates, but includes things like links to blog posts, videos and pictures. And remember, not all content has to be created by you: sharing good content that you have read elsewhere is seen as a positive thing. So, if you have taken the time to read an article and you think it is worthwhile reading, share it with your network. (Be warned though, you will become associated with that content by sharing it—so make sure you have read it carefully before Retweeting it.)

Consistency

Consistency builds momentum. You need to Tweet regularly and be consistent about the subjects you choose to talk about. Twitter is a fast moving community and ideally, you need to Tweet daily. You don't need to spend hours on Twitter, but if you can commit to doing 15 minutes per day every day, it is a good habit to get into. It drives me mad when people say, *'Well I tried Twitter for a couple of weeks and it didn't work.'* You have to be there for the long run. Twitter is an endurance race rather than a sprint; you need to be able to pace yourself for the long-term benefits.

Personality

Everyone Tweets differently—but your personality shows through in those bite-sized pieces and people will have a sense of who you are from your Tweets and the way you respond to other people. People want to get to know you, like you and trust you. By being true to yourself not everyone is going to like you—but that's okay, you will attract people who are similar to you and have something in common with you. It is far nicer to do business with people you like. So avoid being a corporate voice—be your own person.

Measure and tweak

There is no point in spending your time on Twitter with a vague notion of what you want to achieve. It is worth thinking about what business objectives you have for using Twitter and translating those into practical things you can measure, and then track the results. You want more visits to your blog? Tweet with links to your blog and measure the amount of referral traffic you get from Twitter. You want entries for a give-away? Use a special code on Twitter and count the responses using that code. You want to raise awareness of your business? Ask your new customers how they heard about you. Only by checking the response can you tell if your Tweeting is getting you the results you aimed for.

Checklist for setting up your Twitter account

When you set up your account on Twitter, you are given a number of options. You may not know the best way to fill these in. This chapter is to help you to either set up Twitter from scratch or to help you review the options you chose when you originally set up your account. It will also help provide a reference of where things can be found.

The best way to use this chapter is to read it with your Twitter account open and to go through each section step by step.

If you haven't set up your account yet, skip this chapter and come back to it when you are ready to do so.

Do NOT follow people until you have completed your profile. Twitter asks you to follow people when you are setting up your account: follow only the number of people you are required to follow to set up your account and wait until you have completed your profile and sent your first Tweet before following any more. You need to give people a reason to follow you back. A Twitter profile without a photo, a bio and any Tweets is not going to get you followers unless they are your friends already.

Choosing your name for Twitter

Use your own name unless it is really not appropriate. Each business is different, but as a general rule: people like to talk to people rather than inanimate things like logos or companies. Twitter is about people connecting with people. If people don't know who they are talking to, how can they build up a relationship with you? How would someone who knows you look for you on Twitter? If you choose not to use your name in either your username or your profile, you could mention your name in your bio.

- Your username and profile name don't have to be the same. You can use your company name for one of them and your name for the other.

- You have a maximum of 15 characters for your username and 20 characters for your profile name.

- Keep your username short and without underscores or numbers if possible. Longer usernames take up precious space when people are Replying and Retweeting you. They are also more likely to get mistyped.

- You won't always be able to get your first choice of names, and sometimes both your real name and your business name will be taken as usernames already. If possible choose one with one of your keywords in it instead.

- Do not use your year of birth in your Twitter username. Most security questions ask for your date of birthday, so don't make it easy for fraudsters to find it.

- You can change your name and username at any point. Note to perfectionist: it is better to get started with Twitter than spending days working out the perfect name.

- Use caps at the start of your first name and surname @NickyKriel is easier to read than @nickykriel. Twitter will treat both versions as the same username.

How to find the Settings for your Account

If you have already set up your account, you can find your settings by clicking on the cog symbol on the top bar of your Twitter account and choosing 'Settings'.

The Settings option will open with your Account tab visible. Currently the tabs are ordered as follows:

1. Account

2. Password

3. Mobile

4. Email Notifications

5. Profile

6. Design

7. Apps

8. Widget

This chapter will start with the two most important areas: your Account and your Profile, and give you tips and guidelines about the other Tabs.

Account Tab

- This is where you can change your Username. Check to see if a more suitable name is available if you have started on Twitter and are unhappy with the name you originally chose.

- Make sure you are in the right time zone. Make sure the language is right for you.

- Tick the password reset box to add security.

- Make sure you are in the right country.

Things not to do

- Do NOT add your location to your Tweets. This is different from adding a location to your Profile (this will be covered in the Profile section below). The 'Tweet location' is in your account settings. It allows people to see the actual location you are Tweeting from. Do you want burglars to know when you are away?

- Do NOT protect your Tweets. It means that only people to whom you have explicitly given permission can see your Tweets. You are using Twitter as a business tool to increase your awareness so you need to be visible.

Profile Tab

- **Photographs**—It is very important to have a good, friendly head and shoulder picture of you. People prefer to communicate with people rather than companies, but if you want to use your company logo make sure it is legible. The image will be very small. It may make sense to use an image representing your business if your logo doesn't work as an avatar.

- **Header**—The default is a black box behind your picture and your bio. You can leave it as it is or add an image

17

to give your profile more character. Remember that your bio is written in white writing when you choose an image.

- **Name**—This is where you can change your Profile name. Think about how people might search for you on Twitter, would they use your full name, your nickname and surname or your business name?

- **Location**—It is worthwhile putting your location down so that local people can find you and connect with you. You immediately have common interests with people who live and work near you.

- **Website**—You want people to find out more about what you do and your business so make sure you add your web address. If you haven't set up a website yet, you could refer them to your LinkedIn profile.

- **Bio**—Take time to fill in your biography. You have 160 characters to tell people about you and what you do. Make sure you add your keywords. It is worth looking at some other people's bios to get inspiration. This will be covered in more detail in 'Why your Bio is important'.

- **Connecting to Facebook**—Twitter allows you to feed your Tweets directly into your Facebook Profile BUT just because technology allows you to do something, it doesn't mean you should do it. I would recommend you DON'T allow Twitter to post to your Facebook Profile.

Password Tab

Please use a strong password. So many Twitter accounts get hacked because people use predictable passwords. This means that your followers might get direct messages from you offering them sexual advice, a free iPad or asking them if they appear in a naughty video. These direct messages contain unsafe links. So make sure that your account doesn't get hacked. Would you believe that the most commonly used password is 'password'?

Here are a few simple tips to follow:

- Use different passwords for each Social Media site.

- Use randomised characters rather than words—one way to make this memorable is to think of a sentence or phrase that is memorable and use the first letter of each word.

- Use a mixture of letters, numbers and special characters.

- Use at least 8 characters, ideally more.

- Change your passwords at least once every six months.

Mobile Tab

Twitter becomes a lot more flexible when you have it on a mobile device. It means that you can Tweet on the go. It is worth downloading the app to your smart phone and other mobile devices.

You can also Tweet via SMS or Text messaging. This means you can access Twitter without the internet. Often emergency services will use Twitter as a way of sharing information. You never know when it might come in handy so it is worth setting up your phone before you need it in an emergency.

Email Notifications

You can change your notifications in Settings and it is worth knowing that you can change them rather than getting annoyed by getting emails from Twitter. When you start out, you will probably get excited when people start to follow you. After a while, you will want to switch off the email notifications. If you are not using Twitter on a daily basis, it is good to be notified when someone mentions your name or Retweets you.

The only notification I still have activated is when

someone sends me a Direct Message because it is not obvious on Twitter when someone has sent you a message privately.

Design Tab

You can choose a premade theme or customise your Twitter background. If you have the budget to get a designer to brand your background or can use the branding that you already have in some way, then do it. A simple picture can work nicely too. If however, you are on a shoestring budget then I am going to recommend that your Twitter background is not a big priority.

Yes, you DO want consistent branding, BUT Twitter backgrounds aren't viewed very often.

- 60% of Twitter users access Twitter from mobile devices and you can't see Twitter backgrounds on a mobile device.

- If you used Hootsuite or Tweetdeck to manage Twitter, you can't see the backgrounds.

- Even if you use Twitter.com predominately, all you see are people's avatars and Twitter names. If you click on their names, you see their header, Bio and the last few Tweets. To see their background, you have to go to their full Profile.

- The only time I ever look at someone's background is when I check on whether to follow them back or not. Most of my decisions are based solely on their Bio and their last Tweets. If I am still not sure I will then click to see more of their Tweets, but to be honest, I look at the content not the imagery at that point.

- You see the Twitter background when you follow people from their website. There is a brief chance to look at the background before you follow someone.

I have a customised Twitter background now, *but my first 5000 Followers followed me with a standard Twitter background.*

Apps Tab

If you are new to Twitter, you won't have given any apps or tools permission to access your Twitter account. As you start using Tools, this is where you will see which ones you have authorised. It is easy to revoke access to any apps you no longer use or inadvertently gave permission to access your account.

Widgets Tab

You can easily create widgets for your website to show:

- Your Tweets

- Favorites

- Lists

- Search results

Twitter creates the HTML for you to use or to give to your web developer.

If you are new to Twitter, I would recommend you do NOT use a widget until you are consistent about Tweeting. There is nothing worse than seeing a Twitter feed on someone's website where the last Tweet is months old.

Jargon, Lingo, Bots, Links and More

When you start on Twitter it is easy to get confused by all the abbreviations, jargon and shortened links, but the good news is you can quite easily get to grips with all of it.

Abbreviations

You will notice there are a lot of abbreviations used on Twitter. You only have 140 characters or less to get your message across so abbreviations save space. Feel free to shorten words—everyone does—but do be cautious when you abbreviate—as a rule you want your Tweets to be understood, so always double-check that if you have shortened any words your Tweet still makes sense. Remember, on Twitter less is more. Always think about exactly what you want to say and whether you can say it another, shorter way.

Symbols and Letters used for conversation

Twitter is a tool for communicating, you can make a general comment to everyone, but sometimes you want to direct your conversation to a specific person or make sure that someone sees a message.

Mentions or @Connect

When you direct a comment specifically to a person or reply to someone, you write '@' followed by their Twitter name (or you can click on the reply button under their post). This ensures that your message will appear in their timeline and will appear in their '@Connect' tab on their home page. Anyone who searches for that person's name will see your message and it will also be seen in your timeline. '@username' automatically becomes a link to that person's account. This makes it easy to click through to people's pages and learn whether you want to follow them. When you are new to Twitter, it is important to remember to check your '@ Connect' to see if people are talking about you.

Remember to mention people by their Twitter name so that the person knows that you are talking about them. Otherwise, if people are following a large number of people they will miss your Tweet.

DM or Direct Messages

Sometimes you might want to send a person private messages that you don't want to be in the public domain. These are referred to as DM or Direct Messages. When I started on Twitter, you could see your new messages on your home page. Twitter has now hidden them, so that you have to click on the cog symbol on the top bar to see where your direct messages are or visit your profile page.

You will see people talking about sending a DM and all it means is they are talking about a conversation that is private. It is recommended that if you share private information such as telephone numbers and email details, you do so by Direct Messages. Direct Messages will be covered in more detail later.

RT or Retweet

The reason that news spreads so quickly on Twitter is because it is easy to repost messages from people you respect. A Retweet is considered a great compliment. A Retweet is the equivalent of a share on Facebook. It shows support and recognition for the original Tweeter. The simplest way to Retweet someone is to click on the Retweet button under the Tweet. This will share the original Tweet with your followers and will look like the original Tweet, but will have a Retweeted symbol below it. You will sometimes see Tweets from people who you are not following and the reason for this is that the original Tweet was Retweeted by someone that you follow.

If you want to add a comment, it will generally

look like this:

'RT @username: Original message'

Sometimes there is a comment added to the front before the RT or to the back with some indication that you are adding a comment.

I tend to add << to indicate I am adding a comment, other people use brackets.

The RT indicates that you are repeating someone else's message. When your Tweet gets Retweeted, it means that it becomes visible to all that person's followers.

Hashtags

One of things that people notice when they start on Twitter is a strange symbol: '#'.

When this symbol appears before certain words it is a simple way of grouping or uniting topics that people are talking about.

Hashtags are a community-based way of categorising the topics in fields by tagging them. You create a hashtag simply by prefixing a word with a '#'.

For example, if lots of people are talking about *The X-Factor*, they would write a comment which includes '#xfactor'. By typing in '#xfactor' in Twitter's search function or by clicking on the hashtag, you could see all the comments made about *The X-Factor* at that time.

There is nothing to stop you from creating your own hashtags. If you are running an event, you can create a hashtag for the event and encourage people to use it in their Tweets.

Hashtags will be covered in greater detail later.

Twitter Lingo

Here are a whole lot of words that have been invented through Twitter—some of them have even found their way into dictionaries. Many new words are a mixture of a normal word with the letters 'Tw'. For example:

- Tweetup—meeting of Twitter people in real life

- Twibe—group of Twitter users interested in a particular topic

- Tweeple, Tweeps or peeps—people on Twitter

- Twestimonial—testimonial on Twitter

Acronyms

The most commonly used ones are:

- LOL (laugh out loud)

- OMG (oh my God) not recommended for anyone over 30!

- TMI (too much information)

- FB (Facebook)

- LI (LinkedIn)

- RT (Retweet)

- DM (Direct Message)

- YT (YouTube)

- F2F (Face to Face)

- B2B (Business to Business)

- B2C (Business to Consumer)

- YOLO (You only live once)

If in doubt put the word into a search engine such as Google to find its meaning. Don't overuse acronyms because not everyone knows what they mean.

Smiley Faces or Emoticons

Just in case you haven't worked it out :) means a smiley face. And ;) means a wink and there a quite a few other variations.

Actions

Sometimes you will see *a word or phrase* The asterisks indicate a physical action that the Tweeter is doing in real life, for example, *dancing* or *hugs*.

Tip: Write in plain English. The simpler the message, the easier it is to communicate with people reading your Tweets.

Bots

Internet bots or web robots are software applications that run automated tasks over the internet. So watch out, some of your followers may not be real people.

Shortened links

A lot of people who Tweet want their readers to click on a link to visit their blog or website, because what the author says there is not limited by space.

If you want to refer people to an article you have written, a page on your website or a useful article, you don't want to use up all the characters in your Tweet with the URL of your website. Fortunately, Twitter will automatically shorten your URL to about 22 characters. Simply type or paste the URL into your Tweet and it will get shortened for you.

Remember to add the 'http://' to the web address to make it a clickable link. A web address starting with 'www' will look like a link, but it won't click through to the website and it will also use up most of your characters.

- I highly recommend you copy the URL and paste it into your Tweet so that you don't mistype it.

- Remember to direct people to the actual post or web page you are referring to rather than the website's home page. Most people will not have the patience to find the article you are talking about if they are directed to the wrong page. It may annoy them and they are less likely to click on your links in the future.

- When you Retweet a blog post or article, the link will automatically be shortened.

How to write a Tweet

So many people start up Twitter accounts and leave them dormant because they don't know what to say. After you've been Tweeting for a while you forget how intimidating the blank box can be. To a newbie, being limited to 140 characters may seem restrictive. But using 140 characters or less to express yourself can be incredibly liberating!

All you have to do is write a sentence. How long does that take? When you Tweet:

- Write in plain English

- Make sure your Tweet is easy to understand

- Double check it before posting

When you only have a few characters, it forces you to be clear, concise and clever about what you want to say. I always start by writing what I want to say in the Twitter box. If it fits in then, great! I double check it and then press 'Tweet'. Here are some tips to help you fit your message in 140 characters or less.

- It's best to restrict yourself to one

thought per Tweet. Trying to cram a paragraph into a Tweet is only going to lead to confusion. People are not going to waste time working out what you are trying to say.

- Is there a more succinct way to say the same thing? Can you rephrase it?

- Are there any words that don't add meaning? Cut out waffle and extraneous words.

- You don't have to leave a double space after a full stop

- In most cases, the pronouns 'I' and 'me' can be left out without any loss to meaning.

- Words can be abbreviated in any way as long as it's clear to the reader, but avoid text message talk. You want it to be really easy for your reader to understand what you are saying.

- Read and reread for clarity and spelling. It is amazing the difference a 'not' can make to a sentence if you leave it out by accident. You can delete a Tweet unless anyone has Retweeted it and then it is permanent. It is amazing how embarrassing it can be when you see your typo Retweeted.

- Remember every Tweet is public. Do not publish anything that you wouldn't want your family to read, to be published as a headline in a newspaper or to appear in court.

- If you want to refer people to an article or a page on your website, your link will take up 22 characters. Twitter automatically shortens your URL, but make sure you remember to add the 'http://' or it will not work.

Quick guideline to the length of a Tweet

- You have a maximum of 140 characters

- You need to allow space to make your update easier to Retweet. Twitter usernames can be up to 15 characters so, ideally, you don't want to use more than 120 characters in your Tweet. People can then Retweet you adding 'RT @yourusername' without editing the original text. The optimum length of a Tweet to get Retweeted seems to be somewhere between 70 and 110 characters

- So, even less writing to worry about!

Because each Tweet has its own URL it is in effect is a mini-website and can be searched for on search engines such as Google, so don't forget to add your keywords if you can fit them naturally into your Tweet.

Tons of things to Tweet about

'But I don't know what to Tweet!'

This is one of the biggest excuses stopping business owners from using Twitter for their business. When you are starting out, that little box can be intimidating and sometimes, even if you have been doing it for a while, you just need a bit of inspiration. So, here are some ideas:

Join a conversation

Twitter is about forming relationships with people. There is no point in just watching what other people are saying. At some point you need to start engaging.

- Listen to what other people are talking about and add a comment–
  Tweets are public, people like to know that someone has read their Tweet.

- Reply to a question that someone has asked.

- Start a conversation with your industry

peers, potential mentors and thought leaders by commenting on something they have Tweeted about, blogged about or something that was interesting on their website. Show them that you have paid attention.

- Join a conversation by replying to both people.

- Tell someone why you agree with them.

- Disagree with something someone has said (in a pleasant, polite way).

- Find an appropriate chat hashtag and contribute to the discussion.

- Find out whether the event you are attending has a hashtag and start chatting to people using the hashtag.

Encourage people to engage with you

- Ask a question related to your industry.

- Ask a question to encourage engagement —instead of just a statement, add a question like 'Has this happened to you too?'

- Ask for help, the Twitter community love to rally around.

Note: Don't be discouraged if you don't get much response, you need to build up your followers first.

What's happening?

- Say how you are feeling right now. (Be mindful of your business. For example, it might not be appropriate to complain about your muffin top if you are in the fitness industry. It is also NEVER a good idea to bad-mouth your customers!)

- Tell everyone what you are doing right now—I am always surprised how much engagement I get when I mention a cup of tea, but it is good to mention that you are doing work-related things.

- Tell people what you have just done—if you have just finished a workshop/proposal/book, why not share it?

- Tell people what you are about to do—if you are attending a conference someone may be attending the same one or be interested in an event that you are organising.

- Talk about the news that is happening at the moment.

Sharing

If you have taken the trouble to read an article, how much extra time does it take to click on the Twitter icon and share it with your followers?

- Share an amusing article that you have read.

- Share a business-related article you have read.

- Share a thought-provoking article.

- Share a topical news article.

- Share a friend's blog article.

- Share your blog article—you spent time writing it, encourage other people to read it.

- Add a comment to the Tweet about the article so that your followers can see what you think about it.

- If you leave a comment on a blog, find the author on Twitter and let them know.

With your business hat on...

- Tell people about your business and what you do. (Do not overdo this!)

- Share useful professional advice. You cannot give away all your trade secrets in 140 characters!

- By sharing useful articles about your profession, you will become known as being a helpful, knowledgeable person.

- Give useful tips about your business or your industry.

- Answer questions to show your expertise in your field.

- Broadcast the events and courses that you run.

Be a Human Being

- Engage in playful chitchat every now and then.

- Find a meaningful quote that has inspired you.

- Share something personal about yourself that shows you are human, but that is not damaging to your reputation as a professional.

- Talk about the weather (we all have weather).

- Talk about food (people on Twitter have a fascination with food).

A Picture is worth a thousand words

Pictures tend to have the highest click rate of all links. I think that most of us are secret voyeurs.

- Share a picture of something you can see right now.

- Share a picture that will make people oooh and aaah.

- Share a picture that will make people smile.

- Share a picture that is topical or controversial and that will make people comment.

- Share a picture that shows you are a real person living a real life.

Using Trending Topics

- Look at the trending topics and comment on a current topic.

- Join the conversation on a silly hashtag that is trending.

References and Testimonials

- Ask for feedback.

- Recommend people who you know are good.

- Give testimonials freely.

- Refer people to the right person.

- Thank people for writing Testimonials that aren't on Twitter e.g. on your website or LinkedIn.

Remember to think of the person reading the Tweet

- Think of saying something that will put a smile on someone's face.

- Find something that will educate or enrich your audience.

Videos and Presentations

- Share a TED talk.

- Share a useful YouTube video related to your business or interests.

- Share videos and presentations that you have created.

Be Nice

- Thank people for Retweets (RTs), mentions and comments.

- Thank people for sharing helpful information.

- Congratulate people for their successes.

- Send me a Tweet telling me that you are enjoying this book.

Action Points for getting started

- Find one interesting person to follow every day

- Respond to @mentions and Direct Messages

- Find something interesting to Retweet

- Engage in a conversation with at least one person

- Post one business-related Tweet

Remember a Tweet is only 140 characters or less. That is just one sentence or two short ones. What's stopping you from Tweeting right now?

Adding Quality to your Tweets

A great piece of advice by Dee Blick, a best-selling author and marketer (@deeblick on Twitter):

'A balanced & perfect Twitter cocktail...3 parts engaging, helpful & inspiring Tweets to 1 part self-promotion.'

It's alright to blow your own trumpet on Twitter, but you earn that right by being part of the community.

One criticism that Twitter always gets is that it's full of inane conversations. Yes, there are plenty of banal and boring Tweets, but the purpose of this section is to help you to avoid adding to these.

The last thing you want when someone reads your Tweet is for them to think: 'So... what?'
All of your Tweets should have at least one of following intentions:

- Educational—Are you giving useful content that will help the reader learn?

- Enriching or Empowering—Are you adding value and helping?

- Entertaining—Does your Tweet make

someone laugh or smile? When you can make someone smile, you get associated with that warm fuzzy feeling.

- Engaging—Are you having a conversation and encouraging people to engage with you?

- Exposure—Are you making people aware of your business? Avoid being too sales-driven!

For example if you are in a shop buying food and you Tweet '*Am in the grocers buying food*', as a reader I would probably think '*So what?*' But you will get attention if you can add value by:

- Telling me about something that you spotted someone doing.

- Giving me an insight about shopping or your views, such as: '*Hot cross buns at the beginning of Jan*!'

- Asking a question such as: '*Do you find that food evaporates, too*?'

- Amusing me with a funny rant: '*Don't you hate it when they rearrange the food shelves?*'

Always keep your reader in mind. It is useful to check that you are using the word 'you' more than the word 'I'.

Another thing to think about is: What do you want your reader to do when they have read your Tweet? Click, Retweet or Reply? People will only click on a link if they think that there is something of interest to them at the end of it. People will only Retweet if your Tweet made them smile or they found the information useful. People will only Reply if you encourage them to engage with you or if your Tweet has enriched them.

Calls to action work on Twitter.

How to Retweet

The word 'Retweet' has now entered the new *Concise Oxford English Dictionary* which means it is being used by a lot of people. It simply means to share, repost or forward a message or Tweet posted by another user.

Why are so many people Retweeting?

- To share good content.

- To show support.

- To share something that has made them smile or laugh.

- To share something that they agree with or that has inspired them.

- To show that someone has said nice things about them.

- To share something topical or newsworthy.

So how do you Retweet?

On Twitter.com

To share the message as it is without editing or adding your own comment, you hit the Retweet button.

- The Retweet goes out exactly as it first appeared.

- It will have a Retweet symbol below it.

- Your followers will see the Tweet in their news feed even if they don't follow the person who sent the original Tweet.

To share the message adding your own comment:

- Hit the Reply option.

- Type in RT and a space before their @ *username*.

- Copy and paste the original Tweet.

- Add your comment.

Using a Mobile device

- When you click on Retweet, many apps will give you the option to Retweet or Quote.

47

- The Quote option puts the original Tweet in quotation marks and allows you to add a comment.

Using a Social Media Dashboard

- Tweetdeck gives you to option when you click the Retweet symbol to 'Edit & RT' or Retweet.

- On Hootsuite, hitting the Retweet will send the message out as it is. To add a comment you need to Reply and add the RT before the username and add your comment at the end.

Retweeting an online post

- Find the Twitter button, generally below or above the post.

- The headline of the blog post or article will appear as a Tweet with a URL.

- Add your comment to the end.

Retweeting Etiquette

When I am short of time or the person has used too many characters, I will simply click the

Retweet button. I would recommend that you add a comment when you can even if it is as simple as *'Worth reading'* because it adds value to the Tweet.

- You also need to indicate in some way that these are your words rather than part of the original Tweet.

- The normal practice is to use a marker like square brackets around your words. I tend to use << before my comment.

- Some people add their comment before the *'RT'* which saves the need for adding a marker, but I think this can confuse people. Most people add it afterwards.

- If you need to edit the original Tweet to fit in your comment, remember to keep the essence the same.

This is why you should keep your Tweets to 120 characters or less. It makes it easier to add a comment! *Remember: You will get associated with the things your Retweet, so make sure you read the content first.*

How to get more Retweets

Have you wondered why some Tweets get Retweeted and some don't? There is so much hype about how a single Tweet can be spread to millions of people, so why hasn't happened to you, yet? Did you know that there is actually a science to getting Retweeted? That there are certain things you can do to dramatically increase the chances of getting Retweeted? But first things first...

Why should you care about being Retweeted?

When you post a Tweet on Twitter, anyone in the whole Twitterverse can see your Tweet. Well, that's the theory—the reality is very different. There are 250 million Tweets a day, so it is easy for your Tweet to get lost in the noise, never to be seen again.

The chances are that only your followers will pay attention to your Tweet because it appears in their news feed. And even then, not all your followers will see it. If they are following a large number of people or don't check their Tweet stream very often, it might slip by unnoticed.

The Benefits of being Retweeted

- Your Tweet becomes more visible because your Tweet can now be seen by your Retweeters' followers.

- Your Tweet is seen at different times so it increases the longevity of the original Tweet.

- Being Retweeted is a compliment because it shows you that what you have said is worth sharing.

- You increase your network because you are exposed to more people and you gain followers.

- The more times your Tweet is Retweeted, the more it will be Retweeted. People are more likely to Retweet something if they have social proof that it is popular.

- Being Retweeted is a measure of influence and it is taken into consideration for any measurement of social media clout e.g. Klout (http://klout.com) which is a site that measures social influence.

- You increase the chances of the right people seeing your Tweet.

So, how do you increase your chances of being Retweeted?

It may sound obvious, but if you want to get Retweeted, you need to be creating Tweets worth sharing. People like sharing information that enhances their own reputation of being a valuable person to interact with. Think about the last Tweet you Retweeted, why did you share it? Now for the science bit...

In 2009 Dan Zarrella of the Hubspot studied tens of millions of Retweets and normal Tweets and analysed them.

If you want to know more about his research and finding, I would highly recommend his book— *'Zarella's Hierarchy of Contagiousness: The Science, Design, and Engineering of Contagious Ideas* (Publisher: The Domino Project); a quick, but very informative read.

He found that only 19% of all Tweets contained a link. Yet 57% of all Retweets contained a link. He also investigated which words or phrases were the most retweetable. Four of the words in Dan Zarrella's 20 most retweetable words refer to blog posts *'post'*, *'blog'*, *'blog post'* and *'new blog post'* which also shows that sharing a blog post is a good way to get Retweeted.

So if you are sharing a useful article or your blog post, you increase your chances of being Retweeted.

People are more likely to share news and information than conversation.

Call to Action

It is a myth that you shouldn't ask people to Retweet you. Some of the most retweetable words and phrases are *'please'*, *'Retweet'* and *'please Retweet'*. Dan Zarrella found that *'Please Retweet'* or *'Please RT'* generates four times more Retweets than Tweets that don't contain those words. 'Please Retweet' generated three times as many Retweets as the words 'Please RT'.

I have tested adding 'Please Retweet' and it worked for me, but I am sure if you used 'Please Retweet' on every Tweet, it would stop working. So use with caution...

Anyone in direct marketing will tell you that you need a **call to action** and a Tweet is no different.

If you want a Retweet, the simplest way is to ask for it.

Focus on your Readers

Guess what the most retweetable word is?

The word *'you'*. *'You'* is both singular and plural and when we see the word *'you'* we tend to think that the person is directing it to us individually even though we know that it was intended for a larger audience. So lose the ego: Write your Tweets with the reader in mind. The second most retweetable word, by the way, is Twitter! People on Twitter like talking about Twitter. It shows a common reference point.

The least retweetable word were words like: *'tired'*, *'bored'*, *'watching'* and *'game'*. So when you talk about the boring stuff that is happening in your life, it is unlikely to get Retweeted.

Top Tip to getting Retweeted: Instead of Tweeting about yourself, Tweet about something that might be helpful or interesting to the person reading your Tweet.

Timing

The time that you Tweet has a major impact on how many Retweets you get. Retweeting occurs much more frequently between 3pm and midnight and Monday and Friday are the most Retweetable days. Dan Zarrella found that the optimum time to get Retweeted was on Friday at 4pm.

There are Twitter tools that help you find the best time to get more Retweets and *@mentions*. Your click-through rate drops if you post more than one link an hour and it drops even further as you Tweet more links. Dan Zarrella's research showed deliberate pacing allows each piece to receive more attention. So the recommendation is that you don't post more than one link per hour.

Caution: Before you all rush out to start Tweeting at exactly 4pm on Friday, remember that this is a trend. According to Zarrella's research the worst time for a Retweet is about 8am—yet I get a high level of interaction and retweeting at that time. That is probably because I regularly Tweet with the same people first thing in the morning and I've developed relationships. This leads me neatly onto my next point...

Engaged Followers

Users with more followers will tend to get more Retweets, but having high numbers of followers doesn't guarantee that you will get Retweeted. There are people with large numbers of followers who don't get many Retweets and people with smaller numbers who get Retweeted a lot. So what is the difference that makes the difference?

- People with authority—If you are an expert, you might as well tell people in your bio. Dan Zarrella found that people with the words that showed expert status like, '*Founder*', '*Author*', '*Speaker*' and '*Guru*' had a higher number of followers than the average.

- People who interact with others — If people feel that they know you because you have chatted with them on Twitter, they are more likely to Retweet you.

So what can you do to encourage people to engage with you?

- Retweet other people's Tweets—People are more likely to reciprocate.

- Be positive—Dan Zarrella found that being very negative causes you to lose followers.

- Give praise and recommendations.

- Show that you have listened and paid attention.

- Ask questions.

Length of Tweet

The length of your Tweet can make a big difference to whether it gets Retweeted or not.

According to research that Track Social (http://tracksocial.com) did into optimising twitter engagement by studying the length of Tweets, the optimum length of a Tweet to get Retweeted is between 70 and 110 characters.

They found that engagement levels on Twitter increase with length. The rate doesn't change much between 70 and 110 characters and then starts to decrease as the 140 character limit approaches

Anything less than 70 characters, you are unlikely to be adding value in your Tweet. As you get close to 140 characters, you make it more difficult for people to Retweet and add a comment.

So be mindful of the number of characters you use in your Tweets. I suggest you set yourself of limit of 120 characters as a general rule unless you are responding to a Tweet.

To get a Retweet from me: Retweet one of my posts on www.nickykriel.com/blog with a nice comment!

How to get noticed without SHOUTING

How much time do you think you have to get someone's attention on Twitter? If you said fifteen seconds, think again! You have less than a second to get someone's attention: the time it takes to read a Tweet.

There are so many Tweets every day. So how do you stand out from the crowd?

Well... You could choose to only follow people who have a few followers! Your Tweets will be more noticeable to them because their news feed will be quieter. It is ONE way your Tweets will get noticed. But I suspect it is probably NOT the route you want to take.

Put yourself in your followers' shoes:

- What makes you stop and take the time to respond to some Tweets and not others?

- How many Tweets with links go past you without you ever clicking on the link?

- What makes you click on a link?

Have you ever thought about how quickly you

make decisions online? You can only cope with a certain amount of information—in fact your brain is continually filtering out information out all the time. Your brain will only remember about 1% of everything you put into it. Nobody has the time to read everything, so we develop processes to sift through things quickly. If the headline doesn't capture your attention instantly, you don't read the rest! If the Tweet doesn't capture your attention, you won't respond to it and you won't click on the link. You may be missing out on the best piece of literature ever created, but in a split second that decision is made. As you read the Tweet, you are evaluating, sorting, figuring and redirecting information based on sequences and relationships.

So what gets your attention?

Engagement

- We pay attention when we think that the Tweet is directed at us. '*You*' is a magical word because it is both singular and plural. Even though you know that the author doesn't know you, the word '*you*' is very powerful because you subconsciously think that you're being addressed personally.

- Our unconscious mind wants to answer questions, especially if it thinks they are being directed at us. If we find ourselves answering '*yes*' to a question, we are going to at least read the first paragraph.

- We enjoy talking to each other and Twitter is no different. We like to keep conversations going.

Something Familiar

- If we recognise the person who has written the Tweet, we are more likely to read it. Have you thought about the impact of chopping and changing your photograph on Twitter? You want to keep fresh, but if people don't recognise your avatar, they might not read your Tweet. Consistency works well on Twitter and that includes Tweeting regularly.

- We recognise place names because they are familiar to us.

- We recognise patterns: for instance if the headline is similar to a song, or a well-known quote or rhyme we are more likely to pay attention.

Interest

If you are interested in a subject, you will notice when a word relating to the topic is mentioned. The word will almost jump out at you. We have built in radar to pick up on words that interest us. So which keywords or phrases will your customers be interested in?

Surprise

Something unexpected or shocking always get our attention because it stops us in our tracks. Imagine the speed that we are scanning text—to get someone's attention you need to slow them right down. I couldn't resist the headline, '*Do you eat your own dog food?*'

Humour

Anything that makes us laugh, makes us stop for a while. Funny headlines make us smile and feel good and slow down, so we are more likely to read on. There is fun in the pun!

The extra bonus of using humour is that when you make someone smile or laugh, they associate those warm fuzzy feelings with you.

When you use Twitter, stop thinking of it as a broadcast medium and start thinking of it as a way to build relationships.

Remember to always think about the reader. 'What would interest my reader?' should be your number one concern.

Reasons to listen on Twitter

Did you know that half of Twitter users never listen? They never check their stream and only use it to broadcast. How do you think people would react to you if you wandered round the streets talking to yourself? How many friends you would have if all you ever spoke about was you? Social Media is SOCIAL and normal rules of engagement apply. Here are five reasons to listen:

1. To engage

Twitter is a great place to meet all sorts of people and make connections. When you listen to what people are saying, you build up better relationships. Recently a businessman told me that one thing that surprised him since he started using Twitter was that he used to go into first meetings with new clients expecting to do a lot of talking and explaining about what he does. Since he has been using social media, more people are signing up for his services before he meets them! They feel as though they know him through Twitter, they have been to his website and watched his videos. All this before he has actually walked through the door.

2. To hear what people are saying about you

The good, the bad and the ugly. If you come across as being a nice person on Twitter, the chances are that people will start to say complimentary things about your service or your company—and let's face it, it's always great to hear compliments. But if there is a problem or a complaint, it's even more worthwhile listening, so that you can handle the problem quickly and effectively. By responding to comments, queries and complaints in a helpful and professional way, you will end up with a more positive image.

3. To learn news about your industry and local area

There is so much information out there! Following some thought leaders in your business will bring an endless source of knowledge into your news stream. You can't read everything, of course, but you can learn so much.

4. To find out if people have expressed a need

People are constantly asking for advice. If you sell widgets and someone is asking advice about widgets, you would be a fool not to be listening. I asked for some recommendations for restaurants because I felt like trying something new. Many people offered advice, but only one restaurant responded to the question. I was impressed that they had been paying attention and by their personal touch, I had a look at the menu and I tried it. But more restaurants should have responded—they missed the chance to gain a new customer.

5. To smile, be amused and inspired

There is so much humour and so many lovely stories on Twitter that I would be incredibly surprised if you couldn't find one thing to make you smile. It also helps if you follow people who love entertaining others.

Tools to help you listen

To find out what people are saying on Twitter, it is worth regularly doing a search. You can save your searches.
Here are two free Twitter tools that can help you monitor what is said on Twitter

- Monitter "http://monitter.com/" –This lets you set up columns with search terms.

- SocialMention "http://www. socialmention.com" –Real time Social Media search and analysis. You can set up alerts too.

You can also save search results as columns in Social Media dashboards like Hootsuite or Tweetdeck. These allow you to see your search results at a glance.

There are more sophisticated listening tools which charge a monthly fee. Before you commit to spending money on monitoring, think about how you are going to use the information. Do you have the resources to react to the information on an ongoing basis?

Do you know if anyone talking about you or your business or asking for your service right now? If not, it's time to take action.

Who can see your Tweets

Assume that whatever you post on Twitter is public because as a rule everything you post is visible to anyone. Each Tweet has a separate URL and so in effect acts as mini-website and can be found using a search engine such as Google. There are a few exceptions:

Protected Tweets

If you protect your account only the followers that you have approved will see your Tweets. As a business, you would be shooting yourself in the foot by protecting your account. Protecting your account does not entitle you to make inflammatory or defamatory comments. You are still publishing your Tweets even if it is to a limited audience. There have been court cases where the judge has ordered the publication of Protected Tweets.

Direct Messages

These are private in the same way as emails are considered private between two parties. Twitter accounts are vulnerable to being hacked if you have a weak password, so make sure that you have a strong password on your account.

@ mentions

A Tweet starting with '@' will only be seen in the news feed by the person mentioned and anyone following both parties. The Tweet can be found by other people if they are searching for one of the names. It is still public, but not very visible.

If you want a Tweet to be visible by leaving a single character before the '@' it becomes visible to everyone who is following you.

So if you are praising someone, put their Twitter username in the middle of your Tweet rather than at the start.

If you receive a nice comment and the Tweet starts with '@', by Retweeting it, it will become visible to your followers as that person's Tweet. Alternatively, if you reply to it, with a '*RT*' at the front and a comment at the end it will go out as your Tweet, but your followers will see the original words of the first Tweet.

Blocked People

Tweets are public and even if you have blocked someone they can still search for your Tweets. Blocking them will do the following:

- They will be unable to follow you, so your Tweets and your profile picture will not appear in their News Feed.

- Their Tweets using your Twitter username will not appear in your @ Connect tab, so they will not be able to make contact with you on Twitter.

- They cannot add you to one of their lists.

You don't get notified if you have been blocked, but if you can't follow a particular account it might be because they have blocked you.

Remember that just because your Tweets can be seen, it doesn't mean they will be seen. The chances are that only some of your followers will be paying attention to your Tweets some of the time.

Hashtags

Are you puzzled by hashtags on Twitter? It's one of the most common things that confuse people when they start using Twitter. Even people who have been using Twitter for some time can be uncertain about how to use them. They are part of the Twitter jargon and should not be overused. Used correctly, hashtags can be an incredibly useful tool. In this section, we will cover:

- What is a hashtag?

- How to use them.

- Choosing a hashtag.

- How to track a hashtag.

What is a hashtag?

Hashtags were covered briefly in Twitter Jargon, here's a quick reminder:

Words prefixed by a '#' symbol (or hash or pound symbol, depending where you live) are known as hashtags.

- This convention was started by the Twitter community as a way of grouping conversations about topics.

- They create hyperlinks.

- By clicking on them, you will see all the conversations going on using that particular hashtag.

- The search results will include all the people who have used that hashtag whether you follow them or not.

Choosing a hashtag

Anyone can create a hashtag simply by adding '#' to a word. Considerations when choosing a hashtag:

- Check to see if it is already being used.

- Keep it short, it is part of your 140 characters.

- Keep it as obvious as possible. Capitalise separate words to make it easier to read if appropriate e.g. *#SouthAfrica* instead of *#southafrica*.

- Publicise it and encourage everyone to use it.

Using Hashtags

1. Joining Chat

Twitter can seem like a mishmash of disjointed conversations, but hashtags allow groups of people to chat to each other about the same topic.

- There are pre-arranged times when groups will get together and have conversations.

- By using the hashtag, people can talk about a particular shared interest with other people in a group. In effect, it creates a chat room. For example, every weekday morning at 11am to 12pm, small business owners join in #watercoolermoment chat that was started by Enterprise Nation.

A useful tool to help you when you join a chat is Tweetchat.com.

- You sign in with Twitter.

- Choose a hashtag to follow.

- You will see all the chat with that hashtag.

- Tweetchat also automatically adds the hashtag to your Tweets so that other people can see your contribution to the chat.

2. Events

Hashtags can create buzz around events whether they are in the real or virtual worlds. During the event, people can follow all the discussions going on about the event and people can connect with each other. For example:

- If you are going to a conference, an exhibition or event, find out if there is a relevant hashtag. It means that you can start chatting to people who are using that hashtag before you even get there.

- Hashtags are a great way for the event organiser to see what people are saying about the event.

- Using the event hashtag makes it easier to find people.

- Some events even show Tweets using the hashtag on screens around the venue.

This also works well for people doing a 30-day challenge. For example, the Ultimate Blog Challenge had #blogboost as its hashtag. By following the hashtag, members of the group can publicise their new blog posts to each other. Posts using that hashtag get Retweeted.

3. Expertise

Often experts will add a hashtag to show that they are giving advice on a topic such as *#MarketingMoment*, *#prtip*, *#salestip*. By following the hashtag, you can pick up useful information in bite-sized pieces.

There are a number of hashtags used for job seekers and recruiters, so if you were looking to recruit, you may want to follow *#hirefriday #HF* (hire Friday) or *#HFUK* (hire Friday UK for jobs in the UK market) or *#HFchat*. I think you can work out which day of the week this hashtag gets used!

4. Adding Value

Value comes in many different forms and perhaps the most popular way to add value is to add fun— so quite often trending topics will include silly word play. Have a look at trending topics to see if you can spot one. A typical example of word play is used by the many people who Tweet about food (yes, it is true!) and thanks to Sesame Street's Cookie Monster, *#onnomnom* has become a popular hashtag to show enjoyment of food. You can also add value by indicating the tone of the Tweet, for instance, if someone adds *#ironic* to a Tweet, you can tell the tone you should read into the comment.

5. Coordination

Hashtags become even more useful in a time of crisis or emergency as groups can rally around a common term to facilitate tracking. By using the same hashtag, real time reporting of the disaster can be monitored. You don't have to say, 'this is about the news story X' and waste precious characters. Simply by using the 'news' hashtag, people know what you are talking about. It makes your Tweet more succinct and helps everyone follow the news. Twitter can be accessed via SMS or Text messages; this means that you can Tweet without needing the internet which is especially useful in Emergencies.

6. Search

Hashtags can act as tags on Twitter to help you find people and other people to find you. The problem is that some people overload their Tweets with hashtags so there is very little space to add value or to make much sense. Make sure that you find the most relevant hashtag for your purpose and use them sparingly. As a general rule of thumb, you should never add more than two hashtags to a Tweet.

7. Suggestion of people to follow

The most commonly used hashtag to suggest people to follow is *#ff*. And what is #ff? Well, it is called *'Follow Friday'* which has been abbreviated over time to just the initials, although *#FollowFriday* is still used. In theory, on Friday people recommend people that they think are good to follow. In practice, it has lost a lot of its meaning. Many people use the hashtag *#ff* and follow it by a string of Twitter names. There is no indication whatsoever why anyone should follow any one of these people. This is wrong—if you want to recommend someone to follow, give a reason for following them. If you follow someone who is interesting, why not send out **Twitter love** by giving them a *#ff*, but put some thought behind it.

I tend to attract a lot of Twitter Newbies and I know hashtags tend to freak them out, so I use hashtags only occassionally.

How to find out what a hashtag is about

The best place to find what trending topics are about is at What the Trend (http://whatthetrend. com/). This will cover not only trending hashtags but all trending topics too.

Another place to find out what hashtags are being used and to see the popular trending is http://www.hashtags.org

How to track a hashtag

How do you follow a hashtag that you are interested in?

You can save it as a searched item or you can monitor it using a third party tool.

Here's a quick guide to show you how:

How to save a hashtag that you regularly follow on Twitter

- Search for the hashtag on Twitter by entering it in the search box.

- Save the search by clicking on the cog (below the top bar, to the right of the word 'Results for...') and choose 'Save search'.

- Find the hashtag in the future by clicking in the search box.

How to create a widget to show hashtags

Sometimes you might want to show on your blog or website what people are saying in real time about a particular hashtag. Some examples of why you might want to do this are:

- You have organised a conference with a particular hashtag.

- You use a hashtag for a group you run.

- You created a hashtag to show your expertise or your product.

- You organise a chat at particular times in the week.

- You want to share what everyone on Twitter is saying about a subject.

To get a widget for your website is easy; Twitter creates the widget for you. Go to your Settings and look for the Widget tab. You can change the settings, the appearance, the dimensions and your preferences. When you have finished playing around and getting the widget to look the way you want it to, all you do is click on the button. The code will be generated for you to import it to your website.

How to monitor a hashtag using a third party tool

If you regularly want to follow a few hashtags, you might find it useful to use one of the following:

- Hootsuite which is a Social Media dashboard allowing you to set columns for different searches.

- Tweetdeck which is very similar to Hootsuite in function.

- Monitter which is a search tool which allows you to search multiple searches on Twitter easily.

All three of the tools above allow you to save hashtags as columns, making them easier to read.

All three of these tools are free.

If you want to follow a particular chat using hashtags, you will find it useful to use a tool like Tweetchat (http://tweetchat.com) which allows you to follow conversations using a particular hashtag; it will even automatically add the hashtag to conversations.

Do not try to use a trending topic to promote your product, it can backfire on you! Kenneth Cole, a fashion house, used the hashtag *#Cairo* during the Egyptian uprising to promote their spring range and caused a massive outcry. They later apologised for their insensitivity.

Have fun using hashtags, but remember if your Tweets mostly contain hashtags, you are not really communicating, so be cautious. And please remember, don't overuse hashtags, it becomes very annoying!

How to Manage your Time

'I don't have time to Tweet' is a common excuse I hear from Business Owners who say they want to use Twitter but don't get started. And I say to them: But, do you have time to email? To use the telephone? Or to network? And of course, they do.

So how much value do you put on building relationships with potential customers? Very simply, if you believe that Twitter can be an important part of marketing your business, *you need to find the time.* And believe me, Twitter can take time, especially when you start. But using Twitter for your business shouldn't have to take more than fifteen minutes a day. And I bet you have fifteen minutes in your day when you are not being productive? Or, better still, that you have three lots of five minutes?

Reasons to find the time

- Tweeting takes considerably less time than driving to a networking meeting, spending a couple of hours there and driving back.

- In a networking meeting you are limited to the people in the room.

- On Twitter you are not limited by geography or budget.

- There are no gatekeepers on Twitter, you speak directly to people.

- One Tweet is the equivalent of one sentence. How long does it take to write a sentence?

How to be more efficient with your time

Tweet around your work day: Twitter doesn't have to take that much time in your day, if you check your Tweets first thing and send a Tweet and then check Twitter again when you break for lunch or tea or coffee or while you are waiting for a meeting to begin. Make Twitter part of your daily habit like brushing your teeth or having a cup of tea.

To be part of a community, you need to show up and participate. When I started on Twitter I committed to writing a Tweet a day, every day. That was all. I got into the habit of using Twitter every day and it has certainly paid dividends.

Learn to use Twitter on the Go

Make sure that you have the Twitter app downloaded to your phone and mobile devices so that you can use it in unproductive time.

About half the people on Twitter use their smart phones to read their timeline, respond to people and broadcast their messages. How many times have you sat on a train or waited in a queue—with a phone in your hand?

Make reading your Tweets easier

You don't have to read every Tweet! It is amazing how quickly you can skim through Tweets if you put them in lists. If you are short of time, just pay attention to the list that is most important to you.

There are a variety of ways to help you read your Tweets more easily. The most commonly used ones are Tweetdeck and Hootsuite. These are Social Media dashboards which allow you to see all your lists, your *@mentions*, Direct Messages and Tweets in separate columns. They also allow you to update other social media sites from the same place.

Schedule some of your Tweets

I wouldn't recommend scheduling all your Tweets because then you are just broadcasting and not interacting. It is very obvious when someone has prescheduled Tweets especially if they are at set intervals. One of my clients had a problem when one of the Tweets they had scheduled at the start of the week popped up inviting people to learn how to improve their photographic skills at their school. Unfortunately, one of their pupils had just made the news by being arrested for taking pictures of girls in the showers!

Be aware of automating too much, but scheduling Tweets ahead of time is very useful especially when you are busy!

Hootsuite or Tweetdeck

Both these third party tools allow you to set a time for individual Tweets to go out within the free version. The paid version of Hootsuite, which is not going to break the bank, allows you to preschedule up to 350 Tweets. This is very useful if you like planning in advance or if you want Tweets to go out to support your marketing campaign.

Buffer

Bufferap (http://bufferapp.com) is a very useful way to spread your Tweets throughout the day. You add a few Tweets to Buffer. The app schedules them to go out throughout the day. This app is incredibly useful if you tend to read several articles and blog posts at the same time. It means that your Tweets are not clustered together. Research has found that if you send more than one link an hour, you get a lower click rate through to your links.

I used this app when I was doing a talk about Twitter at an Exhibition. In the morning before the talk, I added all my relevant Twitter blogs to Buffer. I told my audience to follow me and that the blog posts I referred to in my talk would be in my feed.

Find your Optimum Time to Tweet

The time you Tweet can make a difference to the amount of responses you get. There may be generalised times when it is better to Tweet, but it is worth finding out your personal best time to Tweet.

If you are consistently on Twitter at a regular time, you are likely to get more responses.

There are applications that can show you when is the best time for you to Tweet. Here are two that

I have looked at:

- tweriod.com—This allows you to analyse when is the most efficient time to Tweet. The free version on this will allow you to analyse your last 1000 followers and will show you charts for the weekend, Sunday, Monday and Weekdays. It is based on when you have the most followers online. However, it only shows you these from 9am to 10pm. It also charts your last 600 @mentions.

- tweetwhen.com—The free version looks at your last 1000 followers and will give you a time to get the most Retweets. Be aware that they give the time in Eastern Standard Time.

I did a test when I first looked at optimising my time of Tweeting. I was shown that around 4pm is a good time for me to Tweet, so I tested it out with a Tweet just after 4pm. And guess what? I had 28 responses to the Tweet, which I think proves the point.

Tip: Think of the times your customers are most likely to be using Twitter and Tweet at those times to get maximum exposure.

Five Ways to use Twitter Favorites

Did you know that Twitter has a 'Favorites' function? Are you using it? Very simply, it is a little star that you can click on your Tweets to show that you like them and want to save them for later.

You'll find the *Favorite* button when you hover your cursor over a Tweet.

Here are some ways you can use *Favorites*:

Bookmarking

The Twitter stream is going past so quickly, sometimes you see an interesting Tweet with a link, but you don't have time to read it. Clicking on the *Favorites* star means you can come back to them later. This is especially useful if you are using Twitter on your mobile and don't necessarily want to read the article on your phone. You may also want to save Tweets that have made you smile or inspired you so that you can refer back to them later.

Collecting Conversations

If you ask a question on Twitter, you can keep track of both your question and people's answers for that particular question. This is useful for keeping it separated from the rest of your conversation so that you can refer to it.

Collating Information

There is so much fantastic information on Twitter, you can collect your own source of valuable articles simply by clicking a button.

Keeping a record of Testimonials

People are quick to be complimentary on Twitter, are you keeping a record of the nice things people say about you? Put a quick gold star on those Tweets and you have a testimonial. If you click on the time stamp you can enlarge them so they open on their own page, which is great for screen capturing. If you don't know how to screen capture search in your programmes and files for the term '*snipping tool*' and you may find you have it on your computer already.

Create a widget for your website or blog

If you are collating information or collecting testimonials, why not share it on your website or blog? Don't forget Twitter has a very nifty Widget which collates your Favorites and presents them ready to be installed in a scroll bar. You can adjust the title, colours and size to suit your website theme. Have a look at the Widget tab in your Settings.

Take a look at other people's Favorites to see how they are using them. If you want to see your Favorites in a format that is easy to print, you might want to investigate Tweetbook (http://tweetbook.in) which will generate your Tweets or your Favorites into a pdf.

Lists are a powerful tool

All these questions can be answered using *Twitter Lists*.

- How do I sort out my followers, there are so many Tweets in my stream?

- How do you listen to Tweets when there is so much noise?

- How did I get on a list when I didn't do anything?

- One of my friends does 60 Tweets an hour, she is filling up my Twitter Feed: is there a way not to see all her Tweets?

- How do I find people to follow?

How to Create Twitter Lists

- Everyone has a 'Lists' tab on their Profile page where you can see the lists that they have created and are following.

- To create a list—Go to the person you want to add to a list and you look for the little head icon. When you click on it, one of the options in the dropdown menu is 'Add or remove from lists'.

- You can either add the person to a pre-existing list or create a list by choosing the 'create a list' option which will show a screen that allows you to create a new list.

- You can call the list anything you like as long as it is less than 25 characters and it doesn't start with numbers. *Bear in mind that people can see the lists that they have been added to!*

- If you want to add a longer description, you can use up to 100 characters.

- Then choose whether you want the list to be public or private.

Public means that anyone can see your list, who you added and can follow your list. Good for lists where you are recommending people.

Private means that only you can see the list. The people who are on the list can't see the list, but they can see the title. Good for lists when you are looking for jobs or keeping an eye on what your competitors are doing.

That's how easy it is to create a list!

Sort your Followers into Groups

There are all sorts of reasons you might choose to follow someone. Why not put them into groups so that you can pay more attention to them at different times? Here are some ideas for groups you might want to create:

- people you know

- people in the same industry

- people in the same company

- people attending an event

- people local to you

- news

- thought leaders

- famous people

- inspirational people

- people you recommend

The choice of how you want to divide your Twitter World is completely up to you.

- You can create up to 20 groups.

- Organise your followers so that you can listen to the groups that interest you most.

- You don't have to put everyone you follow onto a list.

- If you are using Hootsuite or Tweetdeck, you can use your lists as your columns feed.

- You are allowed to have up to 500 accounts in each list, but I would recommend that you don't add more than 200 accounts to each list. The lists become too noisy which defeats the purpose of having lists in the first place.

- Twitilist (http://www.twitilist.com) is a tool that will help you sort your followers into lists. It lets you drag your followers into the list you create rather than add each person separately.

See which Lists you are on

It's always interesting to see how other people define you, sometimes it might surprise you.If someone puts you on a list of interesting peeps (or people) to talk to and you enjoy chatting to them, you know that there are probably people on that list that you will engage with too.

- If you are put on a local Twitter's list, you know that the other people there are going to be local to you. *But be warned: Different people have different definitions of local!*

- Hopefully this will never happen to you, but if you find yourself on a non-flattering list, e.g. 'People to avoid', you can block the creator to remove yourself from the list. This means that they can no longer follow you or see your Tweets and you will no longer see theirs.

Put People on Lists rather than Following them

If you are interested in certain people, but you want to keep your stream uncluttered, you can follow people on lists rather than following them. This means you can find out what people are Tweeting about by looking at the lists rather than you main feed.

- The advantage of this is that you can minimise the noise in your stream.

- The disadvantage is that they cannot send you a private message and won't follow you back.

Follow other people's Lists

You are limited to creating 20 lists, but you can also follow other people's lists.If people have curated a list of people attending a conference, you can simply follow the list rather than having to recreate you own.

- You can follow anyone's public lists by going to their full profile. Go to the 'Lists' tab to view their lists, search through their lists and click on the *'Subscribe'* button and you will be following their list.

- A great source for lists worth following is Listorious (http://listorious.com). This is a third-party site that maintains a categorised directory of Twitter lists.

Search other people's lists for interesting people to follow

If you are looking for interesting people to follow, it is worth looking at the lists of people who you are already following.

- It is an easy way to find people.

- If you know someone through a mutual networking group, the list of people they know may include people you know too.

- I have found some brilliant people this way.

Techniques to help you manage your Followers

Declutter your followers regularly

There are many Tools that help you sort out your followers. Personally, I don't like ones that do things on autopilot. For example, automatically unfollow people who don't follow you back within two days. If you only follow people in order for them to follow you back, you are missing the point of social media! It is good to have a spring clean of your followers though, because some of them may be inactive or only followed you to get you to follow them back. The best free tool I have found for decluttering is:

- ManageFlitter (http://manageflitter. com)

There is more about this tool later.

Twitter and other Social Media platforms

The main strength of Twitter is its flexibility and ease of use with other platforms. Twitter is a great place to start your Social Media journey and works well with *Facebook*, *LinkedIn* and *YouTube* to name just a few platforms. If you are a blogger, Twitter is incredibly powerful for driving traffic to your blog. All the skills that you learn through using Twitter can be transferred to other Social Media platforms.

Twitter Versus LinkedIn and Facebook

Do you approach all Social Media Platforms in the same way? Do you automatically post the same content to various sites? Do you know that *LinkedIn*, *Facebook* and Twitter need to be approached differently?

There many differences, but I thought I would highlight five differences that business owners should be aware of.

1. Formality

On *LinkedIn*, you are always in business mode and on Twitter, you are a person who does business. *Facebook* tends to be more casual and chatty even on *Facebook Business Pages*. When you use *LinkedIn*, think of it as wearing a suit and tie. What would you say in a boardroom or a presentation to a new prospect? Everything is about business. Twitter is like going to a familiar networking event where you know a lot of people. You are aware that you are a business person, but you show your human side, you connect with people on a personal and emotional level. So it is good to bring up the weather, family and sports because you want to find people who are like you. It is about social dialogue. *Facebook* is more like going to a party at someone's house. There may be business people there but your friends and family will be there too. It's not that business is not being done but you have to get the balance right.

Think about the content you are sharing and for which platform is it more relevant. Be wary of using a third party tool like Hootsuite to automatically post to all sites. Twitter uses jargon which is not relevant for LinkedIn or Facebook.

2. Professionalism vs Likeability

LinkedIn is all about professionalism. You show this through providing your experience and skills for anyone to read. You connect with other business people and show your expertise by answering questions relevant to your industry. Everything is available in one place.

Twitter is all about letting people see who you are so that they know, like and trust you. Your personality comes out in less than 140 characters. People get a flavour of not only your expertise, but also how you interact with other people. You let people sample before they buy. For people to get a full picture, they need to go off-site to your website or your blog. People get an impression of what you are like over time. In this way, *Facebook* is similar to Twitter. People get a feel for you as a person.

Make sure your profile is 100% filled in on LinkedIn, you may only get one chance for someone to look at your expertise. On Twitter, remember that you are a business person and what you say also reflects on your business. Do not Tweet drunk or in anger! On Facebook be aware of your privacy settings and how much private information you might be sharing with business colleagues.

3. Expansion vs Brevity

Twitter allows you to say things in 140 characters or less. This leads to abbreviations and jargon and shortened links. The benefit of it is that people can be very succinct and witty in a sentence. I chuckle away to myself reading some Tweets. The disadvantage is that it is easy to be misunderstood and a single Tweet is not long enough to expand on what you mean. To get into detail, you need to produce a blog article, get someone to call you or email you information. *LinkedIn* and *Facebook* allow you to elaborate on points and it is easy to expand on what you mean by sending messages, but there is an art to the short form.

Craft your Tweets so they get your message across clearly. On LinkedIn and Facebook, remember, just because you have the space to expand doesn't mean that you should be verbose.

4. Continuity vs Immediacy

Although Tweets are permanently searchable, they are only visible for a moment in time; it is hard to track back to conversations if you have a busy stream. They need to be repeated to allow for their short lifespan. *Facebook* has slightly more longevity especially on posts that get likes and comments. It is good at keeping the conversation together because the comments are all attached to the original post, but it is exceptionally difficult to search on it. So, if your post has disappeared off the page, consider it to be gone. *LinkedIn* status updates, group discussion and internal messaging makes it easier to elaborate and it can be easily referred back to. An illustration of this: I asked the same question on Twitter and *LinkedIn*. After about an hour nobody answered the Twitter question, yet I was still getting answer on the *LinkedIn* question 24 hours later. I have all the answers to all the questions I have asked on LinkedIn over the years.

For immediate feedback Twitter and Facebook are brilliant, Facebook has a longer timespan than Twitter, but for longevity LinkedIn wins hands down. However, don't underestimate how long people will remember a Tweet!

5. Relationship building

Twitter makes contacting anyone very easy. You can build up relationships very quickly and if you are being authentic, those relationships will build into real life conversations and working relationships. *Facebook* requires both parties to accept the friendship, although it is has introduced subscribing to someone's public feed which is similar to Twitter's follow function. *LinkedIn* is more formal, you have to know the person to connect with them, be a member of the same group or ask someone for an introduction. On Twitter you can follow anyone you want. The one advantage *LinkedIn* has over Twitter is that it is easy to find people that you are connected to because they use their real names and you are more likely to know them in real life.

All three sites are good for building relationships, but you won't build any if you are not proactive about following or connecting with people in the first place and then starting a dialogue with them.

Sharing across Platforms

There are Social Media '*Experts*' advising people to automate their activities. People are being told that it's very simple, all you do is link all your Social Media platforms together and *voil*à, they are all updated at once! I don't mind people posting the same item on *Twitter* and on *Facebook*, BUT and it is a big BUT, I don't think it should be an automated process. Twitter can tolerate posts automated from another account because it has a high volume of updates so for example you could set up Twitter to automatically send out a Tweet for the following:

- Each new blog post

- Each video uploaded onto *YouTube*

- Your *Facebook* Page updates

- All your *LinkedIn* updates

I don't have anything automatically sharing from one platform to another. I prefer to consciously choose what I share on which platform. Whatever you choose to do, DO NOT feed your Twitter into your *Facebook* profile and here's why:

- The frequency that you Tweet is greater

than most people update their Facebook status. Do you want to annoy your friends by filling their News Feed with your Tweets?

- Twitter jargon doesn't make sense in Facebook, if you had never used Twitter would you understand *hashtags*, *RT* and *@mentions*? Not everyone uses Twitter.

- The hyperlinks don't work on *Facebook*. On Twitter, if someone talks about something or someone it is easy to click on their name or hashtag to find out more, plus you can track the conversation.

- *Facebook* and Twitter have different personalities, the users are different. *Facebook* tends to be more chatty and casual. Your *Facebook* Friends are more likely to be people you have met in real life and your family. Twitter allows you to be a business person as well as a real person. Your Followers on Twitter will contain potential customers.

- Just because technology *allows* you to do something, doesn't mean you *should* without thinking about it.

How to make your blog posts easy to Retweet

Have you gone to the trouble of writing content for your blog and you are active on Twitter, but nobody seems to be Retweeting your blog posts on Twitter?

There may be a number of reasons for it, but have you considered this:

You might be unwittingly sabotaging your blog. Here are simple things to check and tips to make your blog posts easier to Retweet.

- Make it obvious that you want your readers to share your Blog content on Twitter.

- Have a Twitter button or two and put these in prominent positions on you blog pages.

It may sound blatantly obvious, but do you know how many blog posts I have read that don't have Twitter buttons? Or have tiny ones hidden away? If I have to spend ages searching for a Twitter button to share your content, guess what? Unless you are an exceptionally nice person and I really like you, I am just not going to bother! Very few people will go to the bother of copying the

URL, going to Twitter, rewriting your headline, pasting your URL and then posting it. Have you missed out because people didn't know how to share your content? Or didn't know that you want them to share it?

Make sure you have a Twitter button on each blog post.

And don't forget that you can ask people to share your content at the end of your blog post.

Have a Headline that attracts the right people

If your headline was your only clue, would you know what your blog post was about? Think of your headline as your sales pitch to get people to read your blog. If your headline doesn't attract interest, you are not going to get readers popping over, even if your blog post is worthy of the Booker Prize. Your potential readers will see your headline with a link. If they were looking for the content you have written, would they know to click on the link from Twitter?

Headline length

If you have a very long headline, it doesn't allow much room for adding a comment or Retweeting it. On Twitter you have space for 140 characters, but ideally you should never use more than 120 characters if you want to get Retweeted. Your link takes up about 22 characters which leaves you 98 characters. Take off another 20 (depending on the length of your Twitter name to add something like '*via @NickyKriel*' which leaves you 78 characters and that is without adding your own comment or call to action. Do you see where I'm going with this?

Keep your Headlines long enough to get your message across, but short enough to be shared.

Check your Twitter buttons

So many times when I have gone to Retweet someone's post, the Twitter box has more than 140 characters, or only includes a link so I have to edit the box for them. Common mistakes seem to be:

- The link isn't shortened.

- The title is not included.

- The blog title is included as well as the post title.

- It adds the name of the plugin into the Tweet e.g. '*via Shareaholic*'. Do you really want precious space used advertising someone else?

- There is no Twitter username for the author.

Try sharing your post using your Twitter button and see how it looks to your readers.

Make sure your content is worth sharing

There are a lot of poorly written, rambling and egocentric blogs out there. *Make sure your blog isn't one of them!*

Write for your reader as though they are in front of you and can hear your words.

First Level–Platform

You need to make sure that your Twitter Account is:

- Completed in full (fill in your bio and upload a decent photo).

- Optimised to be found (include relevant keywords to make sure that someone who is looking for your type of business will find you).

- Updated on a regular basis (at least daily).

There is no point in doing any of the above if no one is paying attention, so the next level is building up an audience.

Second Level–Audience

The quickest way to build followers (without buying them or using an automated tool, which I would not recommend) is to follow people first.

At this stage you will be actively finding people to follow who are relevant to your business. Remember this is an important building block and at this stage the quality of those you follow outweighs the quantity of your followers. When you are new to Twitter, or actively building your audience, you will follow more people than follow you. Make sure that you don't allow the gap to grow too big when you start because some people will see you behaviour as spammy. Later more people will follow you and your ratio of *follow* to *follower* will improve.

Third Level-Engagement

You need to use Twitter to build relationships. The way you measure engagement on Twitter is by how many people are interacting with you e.g. *@mentions*, Retweet*s* and *adding* you to lists. You will know when you build engagement: it is the point at which Twitter starts becoming fun. There are various ways to easily measure Engagement.

- Twentyfeet (https://www.twentyfeet.com) is currently free to use for one Twitter account. It produces useful graphs. It is helpful for looking at trends on a monthly basis. There is a chance that they will stop the free service soon, but it will still be a useful and inexpensive tool to use.

- Klout (http://klout.com) measures your

influence across a few Social Media platforms. Don't get preoccupied by the numbers it throws at you but use it as a guide to help you.

- Kred Story (http://kred.com) is a visual display of your influence and will help you decide which Tweets worked for you.

Don't get lost in the data produced by any of these services, but simply aim for an upward trend.

Remember—Twitter is about engaging and having conversations with people but don't spend your day talking aimlessly; you need to remember you are using Twitter for your business.

Fourth Level–Traffic

Twitter and all Social Media sites are rented property but you own your website and you want people to visit your website. You will get people contacting you for business via Twitter, but they will almost certainly have visited your website to find out a little more about you before they do so. A measure of how effectively you are using Twitter is how much traffic it is driving to your website. Use Google Analytics (or something similar) to measure where your traffic is coming from, the number of visitors to your site and which pages are most landed on.

Fifth Level-Conversion

Ultimately you want people to take an action when they get to your website. If you are generating traffic, but not converting any of it into business, you need to look at your website. What message are you giving people who land on your page?

The measurement of what you consider to be conversion will vary from business to business. It could be as simple as measuring the numbers of telephone or web enquiries, bookings or product sold. When you get new customers ask them how they found out about your business.

I have sold places on my courses within minutes of Tweeting about them, but not all Twitter business comes in that immediately. It tends to build up over the long term.

If you have been spending hours a day on Twitter over a long period and it isn't having a positive impact on your business, you need to rethink the way you use Twitter. Make sure you spend time answering the essential questions that follow.

Questions every business owner should ask themselves

In the past few years, I have worked face-to-face with hundreds of small business owners. So many of them have found answering the following questions very useful and I would recommend you spend a few minutes before you go any further answering them too. They will help you to:

- Fill in or edit your bio.

- Know who to follow.

- Know what to Tweet about.

What is your business about?

Have you ever had the experience in a networking meeting where someone has stood up spoken for a minute and when they sat down you don't have the faintest clue what their business is about? Forget having a few minutes to explain your business. On Twitter you have 160 characters in your bio and less than 140 in a Tweet to get your message across. Can you state what your business is about clearly in language that your customers can understand? People will make a decision whether or not to follow you based on what you have written. The clearer you are about your business, the more customers you will attract...

- Can you describe your business in one sentence?

- Can you say who you are, who you help and how you help them?

- Can you do this in a clear way, using jargon-free language that your customers will understand?

Test your sentence out on a child or a friend who doesn't really know your business and who will give you an honest answer.

What are the keywords to use on Twitter?

You will find the answers to these questions useful when you come to fill in your Twitter Profile and you can use them as a guideline for words you should include in Tweets:

Where is your business based? People often do business with companies because of their location.

What area do you serve? Name all the main locations.

What activity, service or products do you provide?

What words or phrases appear most often in your customer feedback, reviews and testimonials? You might be surprised when you look at the words objectively.

What do your customers have in common?

What aspect of your business is quirky, unusual or unique?

Keep your list of keywords handy and check your last ten Tweets from time to time to ensure you are including them. You wouldn't necessarily use them in every Tweet, but if you aren't using any of them, then it is time to get more focussed.

Your objectives

What do you want to get out of being on Twitter? If you had to choose only one of the following what would be your main objective in using Twitter?

Awareness

Sales

Loyalty

Most businesses would like achieve all three, but consider this: it doesn't matter how fabulous your product or service is, if nobody knows about it they won't buy it. Building awareness will generally lead to better sales. Twitter is probably the best medium for gaining awareness.

Your Customers

These questions will be useful when filling in your bio and working out who to follow and what to Tweet. When I ask small business owners the first question it is surprising how often I am given the answer 'Everyone'. There is a marketing saying, 'If you target everyone, you target no one.' You need to be specific. Answering these questions can help you create a clearer idea of who your customers are:

Who are your customers?

When would they buy your product or services? Is there a particular life stage or time they would need it?

Who is most likely to buy your product or services?

If you had to put your current customers into groups what would those groups be?

Where are they mostly likely to be?

What are they most likely to be doing?

Measuring your success

What does Twitter success mean in your business terms? More web enquiries, phone calls, actual sales?

If you want to grow awareness, how will you measure it?

Trending Topics

News often breaks on Twitter and the place on Twitter that you are most likely to see it is 'Trending Topics'.

What is Trending Topics?

Trending Topics tell you what topics are being discussed on Twitter in real time. The trending topics reflect which new and newsworthy topics are occupying the most attention at any one time. Twitter uses an algorithm to identify topics that are popular right now rather than topics that appear often. Often topics will be trending because of a television or radio show or a news item. Clicking on the Trend will take you to the Twitter search results for that Trend.

Where to find Trending Topics

You will find Trending Topics in the left-hand column of the *Home Page*, *#Discover Page* and in *Search* on the website. It is under *#Discover* on mobile apps.

Localise Trending Topics

The default is set to worldwide Trends, but I suggest that you change the Trend to be local to your country or area. Twitter will also allow you to get *Tailored Trends* which are based on your location and the people you follow.

Participate in Trends

It is good fun to take part in Trends, especially the light-hearted creative ones. All you do is use the exact phrase or hashtag as it appears and your Tweet will be found in search. Be aware that some rules apply to Trends. The following bad behaviour will get your Tweets filtered out and may get your account suspended:

- Adding topic/hashtags to your unrelated Tweet so that it gains attention.

- Repeating the same topic/hashtag just to get it trending.

- Using a Trend with advertising.

- Using a Trend with a request to be followed.

- Tweeting about a Trend with an unrelated link.

CAUTION: Do not be tempted to use a trend to promote your product.

Newbie Beware

When you are a newbie, there seems to be so much to figure out.

Here are five essential warnings!

1. Every Tweet is permanent and searchable

You can delete a Tweet, but if it has been Retweeted or reacted upon, then it is too late.

- Never operate Social Media under the influence of alcohol.

- Never Tweet anything that you wouldn't want your mother or your children to read.

- Never Tweet anything you wouldn't want to appear as a headline in a newspaper or in a court case.

- Never Tweet in anger: step away and reply when you have had a chance to calm down.

2. Double-check your Tweet

Twitter operates in real time and often you will give a quick response to something. It is easy for your Tweet to be misinterpreted or go out with a mistake. A simple omission, for instance leaving out the word 'not', can make a BIG difference to a sentence. So before you hit the Tweet button...

- Check that the meaning is clear.

- Check your spelling.

- Check for typos.

- Check that all the words are there and in the right order.

3. Don't open suspicious links

Twitter accounts get hacked and you will find Tweets in your Messages (also called Direct Messages or DMs) from people that you know but which don't sound right. If your friend is offering you sex tips, a free iPad or says they heard something bad about you with a link, then there is a strong chance that their accounts have been hacked. DO NOT click on the link.

- If you are suspicious, ask your Twitter friend if they sent it to you.

- Make sure your account is not hacked by having a strong password.

If someone you don't follow sends you an @ Mention with a link which seems completely out of context, be very cautious. DO NOT click on the link.

- Check their Tweets.

- If you see a stream of similar Tweets then report them for Spam which will also block them.

4. Not all Followers are Real People

Some accounts are automated to collect as many followers as possible. They are called bots. There is no point in following them; they will unfollow you in a few days anyway.

5. Addiction

Twitter can be very addictive. You may be an addict if:

- You spend hours a day on Twitter.

- You are writing Tweets in your head even if you are not on Twitter

- You get tense when you don't have access to your Twitter Stream and you worry that you are missing something important.

- You check Twitter first thing when you wake up in the morning and last thing at night.

- You read your Twitter stream when you are out with friends or on a date.

Consider going cold turkey if any of the above applies to you or at least consider working on getting your Twitter habits back under control.

Your Personal Brand

Are you trying to hide behind a company logo? If you are still not sure what to reveal about yourself on Twitter, I have news for you:

Being bland, faceless and vanilla doesn't work on Twitter. Forget the concepts of marketing Business to Business (B2B) and Business to Consumer (B2C). What you need to start thinking about is: **People to People** (P2P) marketing.

People want to connect with *people*. *People* do business with *people* they know, like and trust. Social Media is *social*. It is hard to strike up a relationship with a business constantly spewing sales messages. Many businesses think that Social Media, especially Twitter, is just a free advertising platform—they constantly broadcast marketing messages and then they wonder why it isn't working for them. As a business, Twitter offers you a great opportunity, but you need to be willing to show that you are a real person.

When you use Twitter you let people sample what you are like in 140 character bite-sized pieces. People will form an impression about you over time. Your personality shows through in what you say and how you talk to other people. I have had many phone calls which start with something like, 'I have been watching/following you for some time now and I would like to do business with you' from people I haven't even met in real life.

When you are yourself, you attract people who are like you. It is incredibly hard work, if not impossible, to create a false persona and maintain it. It is far easier just being yourself. You are not going to please everyone all the time and that is okay, because it is so much easier doing business with people you like. As the saying goes: *'Be yourself, everyone else is already taken.'*

As a business, the chances are strong that your business, service or products is not entirely unique. But as an individual, you are unique.

Remember you don't have to reveal everything about yourself. Work out what you consider to be private, personal and public and don't blur the boundaries.

Showing your personality doesn't mean you have to reveal yourself, warts and all. If you are having a bad day, step away from the computer or your mobile device. And never, never, never Tweet while under the influence of alcohol or narcotics.

Why your Bio is important

When you set up your Twitter Profile, how much thought did you put into your bio? Maybe you filled in a few words and thought you would come back to it later? When was the last time you looked critically at what your Twitter profile says about you and your business?

Here's why you need to put in a bit of thought when you write your Twitter bio:

Your Twitter Bio is Searchable

Did you know that your bio appears in Google searches? Search Engines will search for keywords within your bio. How many of your keywords (or keyword phrases) for your business are in your bio at the moment?

People search on Twitter

People use keywords when they are looking for people to follow on Twitter. Twitter will suggest Tweets and people that are relevant to the search. Are you likely to be found in Twitter for your keywords?

Remember: Use words that people are likely to use when they are searching for your service or product rather than industry jargon.

Twitter suggests people to follow

Twitter recommends people to follow based not only on who you follow and are following, but also by the words used in your bio. How will Twitter know unless you use the right words?

Your bio may be stopping people from following you

Unless you are a celebrity or a household name, *people will not follow people without a bio*. You need to give people a reason to follow you and what you say in your bio will make the difference to whether people follow you back or not.

Here are common mistakes made in Twitter Bios:

- *You don't give enough information* about who you are and what you do. Don't leave people in doubt about following you.

- *You make your bio a sales pitch.* Most people do not like being sold at. They may think that you are going to spam them.

- *Your bio is very kittens and rainbows.* Okay, if you are just Tweeting for fun, it is alright. But, if you are using Twitter to grow your business, you need to tell people about your business and what you will be Tweeting about.

- *Your bio lacks any personality.* People look for shared interests and humour as a reason to connect.

- *Your bio is full of corporate mumbo jumbo.* Have you ever been at a networking meeting and heard someone deliver their 60-second pitches and still been in the dark when they sat down? Avoid language that appears to be generated by a committee. Speak in the language your customer uses.

- *Your bio is full of spelling mistakes.* You may not feel this is important, but it may be putting off your potential customers and keeping you out of Google searches.

Your Twitter bio should encourage the right people to follow you and also include your keywords. You have 160 characters to get your message across, make it count.

Reasons to Show your Face on Twitter

Did you know that researchers study how your eyes move when you look at a web page? By filming people's eye movements when they look at an online site, researchers build up an accurate picture of what someone actually looks at and in what order. Techie people called it *the user experience* and guess what draws our attention most? Faces! Especially faces of people you recognise.

Here are some reasons to use your face online for business:

You become more recognisable

When I went to my first Tweetup (a physical meeting of people who Twitter), so many people walked up to me with their hand outstretched and said, 'Hello, Nicky, you're a coach, aren't you?' But it was a lot harder for me to work out who they were because their Twitter name was not their real name and the avatar they used was not *their* face. It is much easier keeping it simple.

Eyes follow eyes

A few years ago, I went to a talk by Professor Richard Wiseman_who is both a magician and psychologist. He told us that magicians use a trick that distracts us. We feel a compulsion to look in the direction that the magician looks. In spite of knowing that he was going to look at the hand that didn't contain the coin, I found myself looking at the wrong hand as he did it over and over and over again to prove the point. My brain knew what he was doing, but instinctively I moved my eyes in the direction he was looking. How can we use our compulsion to look in the direction someone's eyes are pointing? If you use a picture of your face with your eyes pointing to the Tweet or head slanted to the copy, people will be drawn to read the content.

Online visibility

Ideally, as a business, you want people to say, 'I see you everywhere'. The more consistent you are about the image you use across all Social Media platforms, the more visible you become.

You even have an opportunity to have your face popping up when you leave comments on articles. If you have been wondering how people get their photo to display on comments rather than a mystery blob, head over to en.gravatar. com. By uploading your photo (it is worth having a good quality head and shoulders picture taken by a professional) and registering the email addresses that you use when commenting, you too can be making an appearance.

Likeability

Do you know that familiarity breeds? It breeds likeability and there is a strong correlation between success and likeability. Recent studies have shown that more exposure is enough to increase the likeability of a person or object. We are attracted to and tend to like people who are familiar to us. Think of the impact your online visibility will have on how people will do business with you and act on it.

Private, personal or public?

What do you look like through someone else's eyes? If you are like most business owners, you will probably have a mixture of friends, business connections and strangers following your Tweets. There is no right or wrong way to use Twitter and how much you choose to share, but you need to **decide where your boundaries are**.

- Which parts of your life do you only want close friends and family to know about?

- Which parts of your life don't you mind sharing with acquaintances?

- Which parts of your life do you want to share as a business person?

Twitter is a brilliant way to build relationships. People can get a good feel for what you are like as a person over time. Here are some tips for when your personal and professional life start to merge:

- Make sure that the year of your birth is not used in your Twitter name.

- Private things should be private and not shared online.

- Do not publish information that could endanger your personal safety.

- Use DMs to share contact details.

- Treat information that you get in DMs as private and do not share it without the other person's specific consent.

- Remember that people can see your conversation.

- Show your personality without airing your dirty laundry.

Look at your Twitter Account as if you were a Customer

What do your Tweets, information and photos say about you? How do you interact with other people on Twitter? Be as objective about it as possible. Would you do business with YOU?

You have to remember that everything you do and say is public. You can still be personal, but remember your boundaries!

How to build a Quality Network

Is there anyone out there?

As a business, you might find yourself asking this question when you are starting out on Twitter. You might feel as though you are talking to yourself in an empty playground.

Social Media is *social* after all and you need people to engage with. It is important to focus on attracting a quality network rather than getting obsessed with quantity. Yes, you do need an audience and yes, the numbers can make a difference, but broadcasting to a thousand people you have collected through an automated process is unlikely to have an impact on your business.

Building a community around you is not that difficult if you follow five basic rules.

Find interesting people first

- Find people you know in real life—for example friends, people you meet networking, members of clubs, customers and past colleagues.

- Find people doing similar things to you. You will have something in common to talk about and without thinking about it, you will be using the right keywords for your business.

- Find local people even if your business isn't local. It is far easier to meet people for a cup of coffee if they are a short drive away and you will have more in common. If your business is local, they are far more likely to pop into your shop or attend a course or seminar if they don't have to travel far.

- Find people who share the same interests as you by searching keywords.

- Find people who are talking to people you know.

Be Yourself

You can tell a lot about a person by what they talk about and how they interact with people. That's why you shouldn't use automated systems like bots to build up your follower numbers— if you automate Twitter you will come across as having no personality. The wonderful thing about Twitter is that it allows people to sample what you are like before they decide to use your services. Your Tweets reveal your personality in bite-sized pieces. You are not going to appeal to everyone, but you will attract like-minded people to you.

Provide Good Content

Twitter works best when you show that you are a helpful and interesting person who provides useful information to others. You don't have to create all the content yourself, by sharing other people's interesting articles, you get associated with that information. Start with your audience in mind. Give them a reason to connect with you. Are your Tweets entertaining, educational, enriching or engaging?

Engage and Interact with people

How many friends do you think you would have if all you spoke about was yourself and you didn't talk to any of them? How do you get to know people better if you don't listen to their conversations and join in? Normal rules of engagement apply in Twitter. Social Media allows you to build up strong relationships with people.

Lose the ego:

- Be seen as a connector and someone who cares about others.

- If someone takes the time to comment

on a Tweet, take the time to respond.

- If someone follows you on Twitter, follow them back (unless you think they are going to spam you or are a bot!).

- Show that you are listening to what people are saying.

- If someone writes an interesting blog post, share the link to it with a comment to show that you have read it.

- Thank people who have shared your posts with their communities or have Retweeted you.

Be Consistent

To be part of a community you need to show up. You don't need to spend hours on Twitter, you have a business to run, but you do need to start thinking of it as being part of your daily routine. If someone asks you a question and you take a week to answer it, they are likely to find the answer somewhere else. Little and often will pay you far higher dividends than bursts of activity followed by long periods of absence. Show up regularly and get involved. You will notice that there are certain times of the day that you get a better response than other times. This is because more of the people you interact with are using Twitter at that time. People tend to have routines.

Where to find people to follow

Start off with people you already know, they will be far easier to talk to because you already know them and they will be more likely to follow you back.

People you know already

- Think of the people who always talk about Twitter

- LinkedIn Contacts (their Twitter name will be in their contact info)

- Business Cards

- Email Signatures

- Search for their name and company name on Twitter

- Websites

- Start noticing the Twitter symbol and clicking on it when you do

Twitter Search function

Use the search function:

- To find interesting people to follow

- To find people in a particular field or industry

- To find people who have a special interest

- To learn more about what people are saying about a particular subject

- To find out more about news stories

- To find out who is asking for your services, skills and products

The basic search on Twitter is okay if you are looking for:

- Someone in particular

- Looking up a trending topic

- A simple keyword

- A hashtag

- Place names

BUT the '*Advanced Search*' feature is far more useful and powerful.

For some obscure reason, Twitter keeps *Advanced Search* hidden. You can find it by first doing a *basic* search. When you have done this, just below the top bar, you will see the words *Results* (for the word you typed), and to the right of it is a little cog. Click on this. The drop-down menu from the cog will give you the option to *Save the Search* or use *Advanced Search*. When you click on *Advanced Search* you are given options to further refine your search. (Alternatively you can skip this procedure by going directly to it via https://twitter.com/search-advanced).

The most powerful part of the Advanced Search is that it allows you find the right results by being more specific about keywords. *HINT: Think in the language your customers would be using, not in your business jargon.*

Don't forget *The Places* section of the advanced search—this is very useful if you are looking for local business. And right at the bottom of the Advanced Search is a little section called '*other*' that is easily overlooked. This gives you options to select other criteria including question marks—and if people are asking for help, they would use a question mark, wouldn't they?

#Discover (in the top bar)

- Who to follow—suggests people based on your bio, the people you follow and who they follow.

- Categories—there may be a category relevant to you.

- Find Friends—this will search your email addresses to see if any of your contacts have a Twitter account. This only works for Gmail, Yahoo, Hotmail and AOL emails.

People you follow

- Browse their feed to see who they are chatting to.

- Look through their lists if they have set them up—people local to you may have a list of local Twitters.

- Look at their Followers and who they are following.

Other useful websites to find people

- Twellow (http://www.twellow. com)—An online directory of people on Twitter. Think *Yellow Pages* of Twitter. It is worth adding the right categories for your business and you are able to expand your bio beyond the 160-character limit set by Twitter. It is useful for searching for people within categories and by place.

- ManageFlitter (http://manageflitter. com) has a good robust Search function within its free version which allows you to search people's bios, names and latest Tweets.

Tip: It is tempting to follow tons of people hoping they will start to follow you, but you will get a higher rate of people following you back if you follow less people but take the time to Tweet them. I tend to follow back people who chat to me, mention my name or Retweet me.

Should you 'follow back' people who have followed you?

When it comes to *'following back'* there are two contradictory schools of thought:

- Follow back most people who follow you

  OR

- Only follow a few carefully targeted people

Which strategy will you use?

- I am of the 'follow-back school' so that I can build up relationships with the people who follow me. I use lists to manage the noise and I have brilliant content and news delivered directly to me in my stream. You will build more followers more quickly with this strategy, but the disadvantage is your news feed gets very noisy.

- The advantage of following only carefully targeted people is a less noisy, more focussed Twitter stream but the disadvantage is that you can appear arrogant for ignoring most of your followers. To only follow a few people is fine if you are a celebrity or are producing great content, but you may be missing out on some interesting people and some great content by doing so.

Either way it is your choice and whichever you choose you should get into the practice of putting your followers into lists.

Guidelines to Following

- Does the person you might be about to follow have a photo?

- Does the photo look suspicious? Accounts with photos of scantily dressed women tend to be bots (Sorry boys!).

- Do they have an interesting bio? I tend to avoid people without bios or with bios that seem to be a sales pitch.

- Does anything look odd in the number of *Tweets* vs *Following* vs *Followers* ratios?

- Do their *Tweets* look interesting and do they have conversations with people or are they just sending Tweets with links?

- Does anything look suspicious in the language they are using in their Tweets or are they showing any other signs of spamming?

If you are following me and I am not following you back, please let me know. Send me a Tweet (@NickyKriel) and I'll be happy to follow you back.

Remember—it is better to build up a quality network than worry about numbers.

How to spot a bot!

I have referred to the fact that not everyone on Twitter is real. There are bots which are accounts run by computers. Some of these are programmed to give basic replies, so they appear to chat. When I started on Twitter, I thought all my followers were real people because I didn't spot some tell-tale signs. Here are five types of bots that I have spotted:

1. Benevolent Bot

These are mostly harmless bots that will basically Retweet your Tweets if you mention key phrases or hashtags.

- Quite often they will tell you they are a bot in their name or bio.

- Sometimes they are used by companies to spread Tweets with their brand or events.

- Sometimes they will just Retweet you if you mention a phrase like *'cuppa tea'*, *'I have a cunning plan'*, *'don't despair'* or *'sausages'*. This Retweeting is random, but it is quite fun to see if you can get Retweeted by one of these bots.

2. Unsolicited Bot

These bots will appear in your interactions and will use your Twitter name and give you a link. *Be wary if someone that you have never had an interaction with before, talks about something completely unrelated to any conversation you might be having.*

Check their last few Tweets, and see if they are filled with @mentions directing people to a link. Don't click on the link—report them as spam.

3. Bots collecting Followers

Did you know some people are willing to buy followers? Somehow they believe that the number of followers is a measure of success on Twitter. As a result of people willing to pay for followers, programmes have been written to collect followers to sell.

If you have used an automated follow-back for your account, switch it off NOW.

Twitter has a rule that you can follow up to 2000 accounts without anyone following you back. Once you hit 2000, a ratio kicks in that you may only follow 10% more accounts than you have followers. This is supposed to help prevent aggressive following. Bots will follow people randomly and when they have been followed back they will unfollow so they can collect numbers.

When someone follows you:

- See what their follow to follower ratio is. Bots will have followed large numbers but might not have many followers. Bots will follow a large number of people and unfollow them a few days later when they have been followed. They count on automated systems following them back.

- They might not have many Tweets in their feed, yet are following large numbers.

- There will be no interaction on their feeds and all their Tweets will have a link.

- At the early stages of collecting, they will have a high number of people they are following versus the number of people following them back.

- If someone has 10,000 followers, but hasn't Tweeted or has only Tweeted a few times, you know they are a bot.

- Bots are getting clever so look at the Tweets. If the Tweets are just random words put together, you have a bot.

BUT remember some people who are new to Twitter might look like a bot, because they might be following people before they pluck up the courage to write their first Tweet.

4. Spam Bot

These bots exist purely to spam you with products that they are selling. They will Tweet regularly with high frequency. All their Tweets will be sales pitches with links. These are companies who have been given bad advice about Twitter, they believe that all you need to do is set up an automated process and if you say it enough times, someone will buy. *Social Media is SOCIAL. If there is no interaction, they are just creating noise!*

5. Real people acting as Bot

Sometimes real people act like bots by treating Twitter as a broadcast medium. They automate their Tweets to broadcast the blog posts they have written or worse still, a string of inspirational quotes. I know real people who use Twitter this way.

I am assuming that you are a real person and that you don't want to be mistaken for a bot—so please don't do this!

It doesn't matter if a few bots follow you, they don't pay any attention to your Tweets and they won't harm you. Just don't follow them back.

Guide to Direct Messages (DMs)

When you start following people, you will start getting Direct Messages or DMs. Some of these will be building relationships, some will be regarding business and some will be unwanted.

What are Direct Messages?

Direct Messages are private and only visible to the person sending the message and to the receiver. Generally they are good for sending details like phone numbers, email addresses and arranging meetings as well as comments that you don't want to be visible publically. Direct Messages are private and it is BAD Twitter etiquette to publish anything that is said privately without the other person's permission.

Who can send DMs?

You can only send a DM to someone who is following you. Sometimes someone will send a DM and you won't be able to reply because they are not following you back. When this happens, I suggest you send a Tweet saying, 'Please follow me so that I can send you a DM'. People new to

Twitter don't always realise that they need to follow back.

One of the reasons that bots follow people, is in the hope they will follow them back so they can then send a spam DM or one with a dodgy link.

Where can you find your DMs?

At the time of writing this book, DMs can be found by clicking on the cog symbol in the top bar or going to 'Me' and looking below your header for the envelope symbol. Twitter seems to keep them hidden, so I make sure I have set my notifications for email and text to alert me when I have a new DM.

Suspicious Links

Many links sent via DM are not safe. By clicking on the link, your account gets hacked and will send out a DM to everyone who follows you. So don't click on them! I can assure you that nobody is saying bad things about you or doing naughty things to you in a video. (Unless, of course, you've been up to something..!) If you're not sure if the link is safe, send a Tweet to the person asking them if they have sent you a DM.

How to send someone a DM

- You can reply to someone's DM by clicking on it.

- You can go to your Direct Messages and type their username.

- You can go to their profile and click on the person icon and choose 'Send a Direct Message'.

- You can send a DM by Text if you have enabled your phone. Just remember that texts allow more characters than Twitter does and that anything over 140 characters will appear as a public Tweet.

Saving your DMs

Twitter doesn't let you access more than about 20 DMs, so make sure you note down addresses and mobile numbers before they disappear. I now use a very economical way to back up all my Social Media sites called SocialSafe (http://socialsafe. net) which allows me, among other things, to access all my DMs. I learned the importance of backing up the hard way when someone who wanted to do business with me got in touch with me via a DM. We exchanged telephone numbers and chatted, but when I went back to my DMs a few weeks later to make a follow-up call, their details were gone! Don't let this happen to you. Back up and don't make the same mistake.

Automated DMs

You get tools that allow you to automate a DM every time someone new follows you. Just because technology allows you to do something, doesn't mean that you should do it.

Why I hate automated DMs

If you are on Twitter and you are sending automated messages to your new followers, then please STOP. Right Now! You know, the direct messages that say: *Thank you for following me... Now Like my Facebook Page... Read my Blog... Give me your email for free stuff...*

If you have been advised to send an automated message to everyone who has followed you, you have been given bad advice.

- An automated '*Thank you for following me*' adds no real value and may annoy the person who has followed you.

- An automated '*Thank you*' followed by a request to '*Like*' your Facebook product, visit your website or read your blog is the equivalent of meeting someone at a networking meeting and shoving your sales literature at them the moment you have finished shaking hands.

If I am interested in you and like you and we chat

on Twitter, then I will do all of those things, but all I have done is click a button to follow you. We don't have a relationship yet!

Human nature hasn't changed. Normal rules of engagement apply. Don't do things online that you wouldn't do offline. Following you does not make me your customer. Often the reason I follow people is because they followed me first. If I am polite enough to follow you back which is my way of saying that I am willing to start building a relationship, don't sell at me. It is just rude!

So, why don't I just ignore Direct Messages? Well, every time I get a Private Message, I get an email and a text. I haven't switched off this notification because:

- I want to be able to have private conversations with people I like

- I get new business through direct messages

- Twitter doesn't make it obvious when you have a new DM

Automated DMs clutter up my inbox and I might miss a message from a real customer. So if you feel absolutely compelled to automate a thank you, please come up with something witty, charming or original. I'll forgive you then, but I would rather you send me a personal DM or nothing at all.

I know I am not the only person who feels this way. The topic of automated DMs raises heated debates on Twitter.

How to stop receiving spam DMs

- Avoid following people who might be bots

- Unfollow persistent spammers

There are a number of sources of automated DMs. At the moment most of the automated DMs seem to come from SocialOomph (https://www.socialoomph.com). TweetAdder used to a big source of automated DMs, but things seem to have quietened down due to legal dispute between Twitter and TweetAdder.

To opt out of receiving direct messages from SocialOomph is very straight-forward:Follow SocialOomph Opt-out on Twitter @Optmeout.

1. Wait for @Optmeout to follow you back.

2. Send a DM to them when they follow you back. It literally can say anything.

3. Unfollow @Optmeout.

This is far easier than getting irritated by automated DMs.

It won't get rid of all of it, but it's a start.

How NOT to get followers on Twitter

Are you putting off people from following you?

Stop Protecting your Tweets

If you are using Twitter to promote your business, you do NOT want to protect your Tweets. The benefit of using Twitter is that people who don't know about you can find you. If you protect your Tweets only the people who you choose will be able to see your Tweets. You have to approve each follow request manually. Protected Tweets can't be Retweeted or found in a Twitter or Google search. Also you can't *@reply* people you haven't approved, because they will not see your Tweets and you can't share a link to your Tweets.

How to check if you have protected your Tweets

Your profile will have lock icon next to your account. Go to your settings page, and check your options for your account to make sure you haven't ticked the Tweet Privacy box.

Twitter validation

Some people use a Twitter validation service like TrueTwit to verify that their followers are real. Instead of simply clicking a button to follow someone you get a DM (Direct Message) to say that you need to validate your account.

It may seem like a good idea to ask followers to prove they are human by filling in a Captcha form, but here are some reasons NOT to do it.

- Every obstacle you put in front of potential customers stops people from going to the next step.

- Most people who ask me to validate won't get followed. I hate Captcha forms, why do I need to waste my time just so that I can see their Tweets in my news feed? And I am sure that I am not the only one who feels that way.

- It is easy enough for a spammer to set up a TrueTwit account which means that they don't have to fill in Captcha forms for any other person they follow. They will be automatically validated even though these are the accounts you are trying to avoid.

- It confuses people, especially people new to Twitter, so they will probably not follow you.

Inactive Account

Many businesses think they have a Twitter account because their web guy set one up for them, they have a link to it from their website and wonder why nobody is following them. Small businesses fall into this trap because they don't understand that Twitter involves communicating and being active. I would suggest that if you have an inactive account for your business, it might be better not to have one at all. It doesn't reflect well on your business having a dusty Twitter account and it is unlikely that anyone will follow it.

Incomplete Account or badly filled-in bio

Make sure your bio shows a true reflection of who you are and that you are not putting your customers off.

Every Tweet has a link

Most people don't like being sold to and a Twitter account with only links suggests automation and an account that is merely broadcasting rather than willing to communicate with people. There is a good chance that you are putting potential followers off if you are inactive on Twitter, but have set up:

- Your Facebook Business Page to automatically Tweet every Facebook post.

- Your Blog to automatically post or Retweet old posts.

- Your YouTube account to broadcast all your activities.

- Every check-in on Foursquare to be Tweeted.

- All your Tweets to be prescheduled.

Not following anyone or only following a few people

This behaviour suggests arrogance to a lot of Twitter people, they think that you expect people to find your Tweets interesting but you are not willing to find people to follow. If you are wondering why no one is following you, but you haven't followed anyone for a while then I suggest you look for people to follow now.

Tip: The quickest way to get the right followers is to follow interesting people first.

Following too many people

If you're following a large number of people

but not many people are following you back it suggests spammy activity. If you are in this situation, spend some time actually engaging with people you are already following. It is also useful to use a tool like ManageFlitter to help you unfollow some accounts you might have followed too eagerly when you started out on Twitter.

Generally it is better to have more people following you than people you follow, it suggests that you have more influence, but when you are starting out you will have a higher follow to follower ratio. Twitter allows you to follow 2000 people before it imposes a 10% follow to follower ratio.

If you follow a large number of people and have a large number of followers, there is a chance your potential followers might feel that you won't be interested in engaging with them.

Not telling people about your Twitter account

Have you added your Twitter account to:

- Your website or blog?

- Email signature?

- Business card?

- LinkedIn account?

- Newsletter?

- Leaflets?

You can't make people follow you but you can give people a great reason to follow you by having a friendly picture, interesting bio and engaging Tweets.

Why you lose followers on Twitter

When you've been on Twitter for a while you will notice that occasionally the number of your followers will drop. Have you been wondering why? Do you take it personally when people unfollow you? While it may be something you are doing, there is a good chance that you will get a certain number of unfollows every week, no matter what you do. It is time to stop worrying about fluctuations in your follower count. But check first that you are not being antisocial on Twitter.

Is it something you did?

- Swearing.

- Constantly selling (nobody likes being spammed).

- Only Tweeting stuff from your website and about your business.

- Using automated DMs.

- Constantly Retweeting other people's Tweets and adding none of your own content.

- Tweeting too often—if someone is only following a few people you might be filling up their Tweet stream.

- Not Tweeting at all—it is unlikely that Tweeting only a few times a month is going to get you unfollowed, but if you haven't Tweeted for a few months, your account will be marked as inactive to people using tools to manage their followers).

It is worth having an objective look at your last ten Tweets and seeing how other people might see you. Is there anything you would change?

Is it automated behaviour?

- Some accounts are automated to follow people and then when they get a follow back, they unfollow because they are only collecting followers.

- Some people use a tool which automatically unfollows people who don't follow back. (Please don't be tempted to use this type of tool. You should have chosen to follow the people in the first place because they were interesting to you, not to get a follow back.)

- Some people might be doing some housekeeping on their accounts using a tool and it is nothing personal.

Is it Twitter?

Twitter will cleanse accounts that are breaking their terms of service such as spammers or bots (programmes that automatically follow and unfollow other accounts) and some of those accounts may have been following you. But you didn't want those followers anyway.

Don't worry about changes in the number of your followers, unless there is something specific that you can change. Remember: You are not going to appeal to everyone and it isn't the end of the world if you lose the occasional follower.

Have you followed 2000 people and can't follow any more?

When you have followed 2000 people you might find that you can't follow any more. If you have reached the magic number you need to start thinking about the following:

- How much time do you spend reading the Tweets in your stream?

- Have you sorted your followers into lists?

- If you are not paying any attention to the people you are following, why are you following them?

- Is it worth cluttering your stream with people who just broadcast at you?

Twitter has rules to prevent aggressive following. For example, you may not follow hundreds of people or unfollow hundreds of people in a single day. This is to stop spammers and automated systems from harvesting followers.

Twitter's Follow Rules

- You can only follow up to 2000 people without anyone following you back.

- Once you have followed the 2000 mark a ratio kicks in.

- Although Twitter don't actually say what the ratio is, it seems to be 10%.

- You cannot follow more people until at least 90% follow you back. So to follow more people you will have to have at least 1800 people following you.

So what do you do?

When you have followed 2000 people and you keep getting messages that you can't follow people, do the following:

Divide your followers by the number of people you are following and multiply by 100 to get a percentage.

If your percentage is *dramatically less than 90%* you have been spending more time concentrating on building up followers than building relationships. You also should also take a close look at the quality of your Tweets. But whatever the cause, if your ratio is close to 90%... *it's time to declutter*.

The best tool I have found to declutter is ManageFlitter. It will quickly show you the people who you follow but aren't following you back.

ManageFlitter makes it easy by showing you:

- The person's bio

- Their activity level

- Their last Tweet

It is easy to sort people by when you followed them or whether they have profile pictures or not.

Remember—some people may not follow you back but they are worth keeping if:

- They are thought leaders

- They are authors of books you have read and admired

- You've met them in real life

- They are local to you

- You have just followed them and they may not have yet had a chance to follow you back

If someone is interesting, it doesn't matter whether they follow you back or not, don't lose them!

Wishing you well on your Twitter Journey

I hope you have been inspired to use Twitter more confidently for your business.

I truly believe that you will attract new customers if you consistently show that:

- You care about your customers. You are knowledgeable. You are passionate about what you do.
- You are willing to help others.
- You are true to yourself.

Twitter has opened so many doors for me and it will for you too.

You are very welcome to Tweet with me (@ NickyKriel). Follow me and I will follow you back. I would love to hear from you. You are also welcome to pop over to my Facebook Page: Social Media for Newbies and to connect with me on LinkedIn. There are plenty of hints and tips on my blog—many of which were inspired by questions that my customers and readers asked me: www.nickykriel.com/blog.

As I finish this book, I am starting work on the

next in the series: this time on using Facebook for your business. Good luck with your Social Media journey!

Acknowledgments

I would like to offer my special thanks and gratitude to Mari Smith for her Quick Start course that got me started on Twitter in December 2009.

To Dee Blick for writing the terrific Foreword to this book.

To The Other Publishing Company for steering me through the publishing process with wit and wisdom and helping me to create a far better book than I would have produced alone.

To Angela Otterson who read every word of each draft of this book, for her sound advice and suggestions.

To Samantha Falconer of Picture Profiles (http://www.pictureprofiles.co.uk) who took the photo used for my Twitter Avatar and the book cover, and David Sewell of Afflatus (http://www.afflatus.co.uk) for designing my Logo.

I would also like to thank everybody who has contributed by adding their useful comments and questions to my blogs and supported me along my journey.

And finally, my thanks to my children for understanding when I am up against a deadline or mumbling from behind my laptop.

Published by

THE OTHER PUBLISHING COMPANY

In the United Kingdom and the USA

Visit our website for our other great titles at

www.otherpublishingcompany.com

Printed in Great Britain
by Amazon.co.uk, Ltd.,
Marston Gate.